Evolution
through Contact

Becoming a Cosmic Citizen

Don Daniels

EVOLUTION THROUGH CONTACT

Copyright © 2012 Don Daniels

Cover Art by Mark Brancucci

ETC BOOKS
Evergreen, Colorado

ISBN 978-1-470063-95-5

Paranormal / ET Contact / Philosophy
Non-Fiction

www.EvolutionThroughContact.com
Printed in the United States

While most pilots choose to stay silent regarding UFO sightings and/or ET contact, Don Daniels is not one of them! In *Evolution Through Contact*, Don writes candidly about his journey from curiosity to experience to understanding. From his experiences with Dr. Stephen Greer and CSETI to his descriptions of contact and communication, he provides an interesting mix of humorous, philosophical, and inspiring stories and commentary that are sure to capture the attention of the reader. In addition, each chapter is enhanced with links to informational resources, a chapter exercise (designed to enhance your personal understanding and experience with the topics in the chapter), and poems by the author.

Have you ever wondered, much less even known about, what you should do if you were psychotronically attacked? What ET communication is really like? The how's and why's—and importance—of creating an egregore? What happened behind the scenes during and after the Disclosure Project presentation at the National Press Club? What was commonly misunderstood about the Condon Report? What openness gets you when you're a commercial pilot? How you can prepare yourself for contact? Or how OOBE (Out of Body Experience) relates to extraterrestrial contact? If you're preparing to read "just another book" on the subject, prepare yourself, instead, to expect the unexpected as this book takes YOU on a journey of personal discovery.

Sandy Jones, Consultant, Coach, and
Dolores Cannon Hypnotherapist

Very interesting reading and I like the exercises at the end of the chapters. You just can't read and put it down, you get something to do.

Heidi Moller

Loved your open, friendly, humorous style.

Monique Kesos

Don Daniels takes the high road in *Evolution through Contact*, everything about his experiences lends a very positive note to the whole subject of extraterrestrial contact. I'll recommend it to friends who are dragging their feet about the larger picture.

Mark Kimmel
Author, Teacher & Channel
Cosmic Paradigm

They were definitely not human.

In fact, they were not even mammalian.

They were all around me,

and they were touching me gently,

like a blind person feeling someone's face...

FOREWORD

A chance conversation with the author of this book caused me to recall my first UFO sighting which occurred about sixteen years ago. It was a clear night, and I was just wrapping up my shift working the complaint desk of a police department in the San Francisco Bay Area. I had received approximately four phone calls from bewildered citizens who each cited a big bright light hovering some distance above them. The reports were merely shrugged off as nonsense by our dispatchers, and the duty sergeant hypothesized that people were just noticing the bright lights of the fishing vessels. During my drive home I saw the bright steady single light at twenty degrees above the city's skyline. It was not an aircraft and definitely not a police helicopter's spotlight. It hovered and then suddenly dashed about the sky like no conventional aircraft possibly could before it disappeared. Much to my chagrin, I was rather nonchalant about the sighting. However, it did cause me to realize that we were probably not alone in this universe. The myriad of questions that stemmed from that moment remained un-entertained until I came across the author and this book.

Evolution Through Contact helped me understand that there are others who have experienced the extraordinary. The book presented such a refreshing take on the subject. Don Daniels is a credible professional who speaks of his evolutionary experience boldly for the sake of others. The experiences shared by the author exemplify how the universe is a mystery waiting to be discovered, and he has assumed a strong role as a proponent for the official disclosure of extraterrestrial existence. Furthermore, the experiences shared are testaments that we have much room left to grow into our role as galactic citizens. *Evolution Through Contact* is an engaging, intelligent, and thought-provoking read, which will surely challenge our thoughts on religion, government, and science. For the open-minded reader, this book also serves as a compelling introduction to a far more interesting universe.

Patrick Magalang
Airline Captain

TABLE OF CONTENTS

PREFACE

This book started out as a simple How-To on preparing yourself mentally, emotionally, and psychologically for your own ET Contact experiences, and some suggestions on how to attempt to initiate your own contacts when you were ready. However, in the writing this book has evolved into something much more important, a treatise on Becoming a Cosmic Citizen.

There are many indications that 2012 will be a pivotal year in human evolution, a time when many—if not most of us—will move into a fourth dimensional way of being, one that is Love and Oneness based. There are also some who have consciously chosen darkness, hate, fear and greed, and they have free will to continue in a third dimensional fear-based world to continue learning those lessons.

Then there is a significant portion of the population who are still asleep, unaware of the epic decisions that will be upon us in the very near future. If you have friends and loved ones in that category, and you like the messages I share, then perhaps passing this book on to them can help awaken them to the possibilities before them.

Each person has to decide for themselves whether to personally ascend or to remain in the familiar fear-based world of separation and limited consciousness. It is a bold leap to move into a world that is love and oneness based, fully conscious and enlightened, but it will be very rewarding.

There will be other opportunities in the future, but the energies for enlightenment and moving into Full Consciousness will not be this strong again for a very long time. The best you can do is offer enlightenment and encouragement while respecting each individual's free will to choose their own path.

This book relates many of my own personal experiences, but the journey should be even more about you than it is about me. There are many suggestions and concepts offered that will help you move towards Cosmic Citizenship in your own right.

If you bought this book because you are interested in having your own personal Extraterrestrial Contact experiences, place yourself in my shoes as the events occur and feel how YOU would react. Then use the chapter exercises to improve your thoughts and reactions so that they would be proper and appropriate for your own peaceful contact experience. I've been there, done that. This book is about helping you to do likewise in a safe and comfortable manner.

If you bought this book to try to find closure with some experience you have had in the past, there are a number of people who have already found clarity and comfort from what you will learn here. Hopefully it will help you in that respect also. In fact, this book has changed lives already. Almost everyone who has previewed **Evolution Through Contact** has told me that it gave them comfort and insight, and changed their outlook for the better. It is guaranteed to give you a new perspective on our place in the universe and even change the way you look at your fellow travelers on this Earth adventure.

Be ready for some high strangeness and astounding synchronicities, because there are no coincidences. As you prepare yourself mentally, emotionally, and psychologically for exploration into the larger realities, you will be given signs that you are making progress. For us sometimes these synchronistic events became so common that we would just smile and say, "Well, there was another one!" We came to expect and look forward to the high strangeness, and revel in what we could learn from it.

The recommendations contained within this book were gleaned from several sources and mostly from 12 years of my own personal journey. If you follow my advice and honestly work on preparing yourself in the ways that I suggest, it is my belief that you will greatly increase your chances of peaceful encounters with our cosmic neighbors even before Open Contact is officially declared, as well as being ready to step into a leadership or teaching role when open contact is announced. Your efforts will be noticed and appreciated, and you will be given experiences at the rate that you are ready for them. The only thing that can stop you is fear, ego, or greed.

You do not need to travel to anywhere special to have contact experiences, for it is not where you are physically, but where you are mentally, emotionally, spiritually and psychologically that matters most. You can have contact in your own home in the middle of a major city. You may be more likely to see a UFO if you get out into more rural or remote areas where you are in nature and the sky is dark and clear. You will also find that there is a beautiful spiritual aspect to meditating out under the stars that can help facilitate your progress. Going out in nature with a small group provides mutual support and a commonality of purpose that makes it easier to meet whatever high strangeness you encounter with courage and great joy.

Most of all have fun with it, as now is the time for humanity to go out and become cosmic citizens. There is so much to explore and endless adventures await you in the Cosmos.

Don Daniels

ACKNOWLEDGMENTS

I would like to thank all who have helped on this project over the past several years. Their input and suggestions helped make sure this book achieve its primary objectives, understanding our place in the universe. It is also intended to help people who are interested prepare for their own ET contact experiences, and help those who have already had such experiences find peace and meaning in them.

My very special thanks to Sierra Neblina for trusting me enough to share her very unusual experiences with me, and trusting my advice enough to find peace with what has happened to her. In a way it allowed me a test case to prove that what had worked for me will also work well for others. Sierra is now counseling others who have had contact experiences, and really finding her power to control and continue her ongoing contact experiences. She is now proceeding with her mission to share her experiences and help educate the rest of us as to the changes that are coming. It has been a pleasure getting to know her better and to be working toward the same goals in our own ways. Thanks, Sierra, for allowing me to be a friend.

Thanks to Shirley Morgan for her help with editing and breaking my paragraph long sentences down into more readable form.

Phil Catalano, Mark Kimmel, Sandy Jones, Alan Moses, Patrick Magalang, Karen Ong, Heidi Moller and Monique Kesos for their reviews and comments.

The students and staff of the Youngstown State University Psychology class: *"Extraterrestrials, Meditation and Free Energy"* who used parts of my book in their class and then interviewed me via a Skype Conference. Their enthusiasm encouraged me to finish the project.

I would also like to thank all my friends who encouraged me to keep going when the learning curve of writing a book, with all the related details, seemed overwhelming.

Thanks to Annie Miller at Earth Star Publications, who took my amateur formatting and layout and turned this book into a professional looking product.

Last, I would like to give special thanks to Mark Brancucci, whose cover artwork so beautifully captures the essence of humankind becoming cosmic citizens.

HOW QUICKLY IT BECOMES REAL

Up until my first week in the desert with CSETI[1] in 1999, UFOs had remained an intellectual curiosity, but not a personal experience. That was about to change, in a big way! The very first night in the field I went from believing to **Knowing!**

It was a dark and moonless night in the Baca[2]. At nearly 8000 feet elevation and over 40 miles from the nearest city of any significant size, the stars seem to leap out of the black sky. The Milky Way was resplendent in its brilliance, not washed out like it is near larger cities. You really feel like you are out there among them.

Early in the evening a number of us saw an object that looked kind of like a large meteor (but not quite) streaking down at an angle in the southwest sky. It was more of a smudgy energy streak than a point with a spreading tail, this being the factor which first really caught my eye. Then it made an abrupt, almost instantaneous stop about 20 degrees above the horizon. It was immediately a large blue-white point of light in the night sky, significantly bigger and brighter than Venus. I stated the obvious: **"That's no meteor!"**

It is very difficult to estimate distance to a point of light in the night sky, especially when you have no idea how big it is. We guessed it was somewhere over the San Luis valley, anywhere from 2 to 20 miles away. Dr. Greer[3] then picked up his laser pointer and flashed twice. The "Craft" flashed back twice. **Cool!** Someone else in the group picked up a million candle power spotlight, and repeated the experiment. They

---

[1] CSETI: The Center for the Study of Extraterrestrial Intelligence. www.cseti.org

[2] The Baca is the high desert near the Great Sand Dunes National Monument in the San Luis Valley, Colorado.

[3] International director of CSETI

responded in kind.

Being a pilot I knew better than most what this meant. We do it at times when we are flying at night, see another aircraft, and flash our landing lights at them. It is basically a form of non-verbal communication where we are saying "Hi! I see you." If they respond, we know that they also see us, and we are watching out for each other.

What had we just done? In this case we had initiated non-verbal communications with what appeared to be an Extraterrestrial Spacecraft, said Hi, and the occupants had said Hi back! This is profound, and much better than simply passively observing an anomalous craft. While I knew that our covert guys had some pretty impressive reverse-engineered technology, I also didn't think the covert humans would be making their presence known and "conversing" with us in a friendly way. They would most likely be trying to avoid detection or to scare us.

After this initial exchange, I was going to suggest that we try flashing a prime number sequence[4], and see if we could alternate numbers once the pattern became obvious. But before I could propose that, Dr. Greer suggested we try to Remote View[5] the craft and its occupants and see if we could establish a higher level of telepathic contact. My Rosicrucian[6] training was most helpful here, having already given me the basics of meditation, an overview of telepathy, and other truly NORMAL abilities that we all possess. Before we could get started on the Remote Viewing, a pale blue-white beam of light about the color of faded blue jean material projected from the craft and formed a forty foot diameter circle on our group of eighteen researchers. Then a faint scan line moved through the beam, and finally the beam shortened up, not cutting off like when we turn off a searchlight, but actually retracting back into the craft. It was a really weird effect, one I have no idea how they accomplished. I

---

[4] Numbers that can only be divided by one and themselves: 1, 2, 3, 5, 7, 11, 13, 17, 19, 23...

[5] Remote Viewing is a meditative technique whereby you extend your consciousness beyond your physical body in order to "see" or gain impressions from a remote location in space and or time. See Appendix A for a Remote Viewing exercise you can try yourself.

[6] Rosicrucian Order, AMORC (Ancient Mystical Order Rosae Cruces) http://www.rosicrucian.org

said, **"Cool, we've just been scanned!"** It was so obvious! It also occurred to me that the occupants of that craft probably knew more about me than I knew about me at that particular moment. While that thought was a bit intimidating, since my intentions were pure I did not feel in any way threatened by it. This was my first night out in the field, I had experienced **My First Contact**, and it had been a pretty darn good one at that!

Those of you who have ever been in an earthquake will have some idea of how I felt about that time. You take the ground for granted as being granite. While you know intellectually that earthquakes can happen, when something that has been the bedrock of your experience suddenly moves violently beneath your feet, it leaves you a little off balance and with just a bit of a hollow feeling in the pit of your stomach. We certainly felt that way after the 1989 World Series earthquake in the San Francisco Bay area. Emotionally you start to question some of your basic assumptions in life, and look at many things from a new perspective. I thought I was pretty intellectually and psychologically prepared for whatever might happen on the UFO Research Outing, but just as in an earthquake, when it actually happens your whole paradigm is shifted. Suddenly my understanding and beliefs about UFOs had been shifted from Belief to a nearly certain Knowing, and it was like my whole psyche had taken a bit of a lurch.

As I lay in bed that night reviewing the events of the evening and analyzing what had happened, I went over quite a number of different scenarios trying to explain what had happened. **WHO** is this Dr. Greer? Is this for real or is he just a very good con artist? Could it be a covert human craft and if so, why would they interact with us the way they did? Did we really just say Hi to some extraterrestrials that had dropped in to visit us, and did they respond to our lights and say Hello back?

A lot of the movies, TV and other media, and even UFO "researchers" talk about the "Evil Aliens" out to abduct or enslave us, but this had seemed like a pretty friendly exchange. Perhaps Dr. Greer is right about the peaceful paradigm, and most of the rest is just fear, paranoia, misinterpretation, or disinformation. Wow! Did this really happen or am I just deluding myself? I needed to understand what I had just witnessed. Everyone else in the group had seen it too, and had described the same events, so if it was delusion it was a mass delusion. I had a hard time getting to sleep that night because for hours all kinds of thoughts were ricocheting around like crazy inside my head.

On later outings we have seen craft make a giant S-turn from what appeared to be Satellite altitude down into the Great Sand Dunes[7] in a manner of a couple of seconds, where it just winked out as it appeared to fly right into or through the ground. We have also seen "Satellites" make 90 or 180 degree instantaneous turns, as well as a wide variety of other unusual phenomena. Over the years since then, I have had so many sightings that I have run out of fingers and toes to count them.

---

[7] There is an interesting note about Mt Blanca and the Great Sand Dunes near Alamosa Colorado. For a long time the geologists have been trying to determine where the sand came from. Their two main theories are that it came from the west with the prevailing winds and collected in the pocket in the Sangre de Cristo mountain range. The opposing theory is that the sand came over the top of the mountains and collected in the back swirl of wind. Geologists have analyzed the magnetite composition of the sand but it's composition does not match sand either east or west of the dunes. I also find it interesting that there are no dunes in similar portions of the mountain range to the north or south.

The Southwest Indians referred to Mt. Blanca as the Sacred Mountain of the East, the mountain of **Knowledge.** The San Luis Valley was referred to as the "Bloodless Valley," as no violence was permitted amongst the Indians of different tribes who were on their pilgrimages to the Mountain of Knowledge. The anomalous Great Sand Dunes are just north of Mt. Blanca and the Native Americans say that the dunes were formed when the **Ant People** hollowed out Mt. Blanca. Hmm! Ant People in a hollow mountain, known as the mountain of knowledge, makes one wonder who was imparting that knowledge.

CHAPTER EXERCISE: BASIC MEDITATION

Being able to attain a higher state of consciousness is very helpful in trying to achieve contact. If you do not have a meditation practice, I suggest you research one or try this simple breathing technique.

Get seated comfortably, preferably in a firm relatively upright chair, separate your feet, and place your hands on your legs, palms down. For energy flow in this posture it is preferable that your hands or feet don't cross each other. Alternatively, you can sit on a small pillow on the floor with your legs crossed if that is more comfortable for you. Inhale slowly and deeply, and pause for as long as it is comfortable, and then exhale slowly and completely, and pause for as long as comfortable. Focus on your breath, feel it going into and out of your body. Continue this for several minutes and you will notice a moment of deep profound silence that occurs in the pause between the breaths. As you become aware of that silence, move into it, and try to gradually expand that state until gradually it exists throughout the entire breath cycle. Now, while in that deep silence, *become aware of awareness itself*, not the sounds which you hear, but *that* by which you are *able* to hear, to be aware, and to perceive. Rather than fighting off the distraction of the sounds around you, consider them an example of your ability to perceive, and then move on to ponder how it is that we are able to perceive.

If this technique doesn't work for you or if you want to try a different technique, there are many meditation courses taught. Check with your YMCA or local Buddhist community, or look for Transcendental Meditation courses. Sometimes Metaphysical Bookstores will have courses or can recommend one, or even recommend a good book. If one discipline doesn't work well for you, try another. Prices may vary considerably, so I suggest simply trying this breathing technique to help focus and quiet the mind, and to become receptive to intuition and insight. In later chapters I will expand on this technique and show you how to use it for different purposes. For now, just set aside 20-30 minutes free from distractions several times a week to practice this technique. After five or ten sessions, you will most likely find some very interesting things starting to happen as you begin to increase your attunement.

IN THE BEGINNING

As a child I was always interested in things that flew. My first word was "Car" while standing on the couch looking out the window and pointing at a car. This was followed shortly by "Plane," also associated with the object. This blew my parents away that I was associating the word and the object right away. Mama and Dada followed soon afterward, much to my parents' relief. Things that flew continued to play a big part in my early years, be it paper airplanes, balsa wood gliders and rubber band powered planes, kites, line control model airplanes, and later radio control airplanes.

My first thoughts that I remember about UFOs and Extraterrestrials were in the 6th grade. I had a rather boring teacher, and when I wasn't challenging her on some point of scientific fact[8], the environment tended to foster my tendency to daydream. One of my common daydreams was of a flying saucer landing on the schoolyard, and my going out to meet the occupants. I thought that would be very cool, and I don't recall ever having any fear about such an encounter.

I don't know what prompted this daydream other than having a father who was rather open minded and discussed such issues and possibilities as UFOs with us. I suppose it is possible that I had some earlier contact, either on a physical or telepathic level, but to this date I have no conscious memory of such. I have also been reluctant to do any hypnotic regression as there are too many opportunities for a poorly trained hypnotherapist to actually implant false memories through suggestion (either intentionally or unintentionally), and I did not want to take a chance of tainting my memories.

---

[8] Our science text books were at least 10-20 years old, and I had my own subscription to *Science Newsletter*, so I would often correct something she taught us. I would bring in the appropriate copy of *Science Newsletter* the next day to show the teacher I was right. Unfortunately, at that time I did not understand the social grace of not publicly correcting and thus embarrassing the teacher in class. I hope she has forgiven my pursuit of truth in all cases.

As a kid I was a voracious consumer of Science Fiction, and in 6th grade the grade school librarian had to borrow books from the Jr. High library to keep up with my request. She told me I was reading at an 8th-9th grade level at that time. I just couldn't get enough of the new and mind-expanding concepts. Some of my favorite authors at the time were Arthur C. Clark, Allen E. Norris, and Robert Heinlein. I definitely remember reading *Raiders from the Rings* by Allen E. Norris in the 6th grade, and was impressed by the non-lethal Tangle Guns that shot a gooey tangled net that wrapped around the target to immobilize someone without hurting them.

In Jr. High I started flying real airplanes, taking some formal lessons in my Dad's Cessna 206 when I was 14. This was so that I would be a more fully qualified Co-Pilot on family trips and be able to land the plane myself if the need ever arose. I knew from even that time that I wanted to be a professional pilot, and my life and education were centered upon that goal.

On my 16th birthday, (the youngest you can solo[9] a powered plane) I got up early, rode my bicycle to the airport, and went flying with my instructor. We had planned for an attempt to solo that day, so I was a bit over prepared. Just to add to the pressure a little, the local newspaper reporter showed up to photograph and report the event. Thanks, Mom! The weather cooperated, and on February 26, 1968 the

---

[9] To fly solo means to fly all by yourself, hence first solo is the first time you fly an airplane all by yourself without an instructor on board with you.

instructor got out and I took flight alone for the first time, making three solo trips around the traffic pattern.

That was a Tuesday, and the drivers licensing office was only open Tuesdays and Thursdays in our small town, so I waited until Thursday to go take my driving test. I had my priorities!

Later on as I progressed in my flying, I started work as a flight instructor in Boise, Idaho. I greatly enjoyed teaching and watching the students' faces light up as they got the concepts I was trying to teach. Sharing my love of flying with others was as enjoyable as flying myself. Whenever I would solo a student at the Boise airport, I would run up to the control tower (this was way pre-9/11) to watch from that vantage point, and visit with the tower controllers. I got to know them pretty well, and around this time another "fantasy" emerged. I did some flying in the Idaho Back Country, and I got to thinking that it would be really neat if I encountered a Flying Saucer at one of the remote backcountry airstrips, and was able to exchange flying lessons with the occupants. After we learned each other's craft, I would contact Boise Tower inbound in an "Experimental" craft, and after landing the Flying Saucer right in front of the tower, I would inform the tower that I had a student inbound in a few minutes in my Cessna 140[10], and his English wasn't real good. I had a lot of fun with that daydream, but it was always the love of flying and the common bond of aviators of all types that was the overriding theme.

Since that time I have flown over 50 models of single engine and light twin engine aircraft, Sailplanes (gliders), Amphibious Seaplanes, as well as a few hours in a Helicopter and a Hot Air Balloon. I have also flown many thousands of hours in Boeing 727, 737, 757, 767, and most recently the Boeing 777 flying international routes, but I would still love to learn how to fly one of those round disk things. Something in my aviation career still feels incomplete.

---

[10] My Cessna 140 was a 2 seat taildragger built in 1946, purchased used by me in the early 70's, rebuilt with the assistance of an aircraft mechanic in my garage and later his garage. We later upgraded it from a Continental 85 HP engine to a Lycoming 130 HP engine, that engine we later overhauled in the living room of our apartment in Alameda California. We had a lot of fun in that little bird.

CHAPTER EXERCISE: LIFE REVIEW

Take a little time over the next few days, preferably in meditation, to review and reflect on how your childhood may have prepared you for Extraterrestrial Contact. Conversely, consider how your experiences may have indoctrinated you with beliefs that may be hindrances you will have to overcome. Have scary movies implanted a subconscious fear response with regard to a potential meeting with extraterrestrials, or has a positive movie like the ORIGINAL *The Day the Earth Stood Still, ET, Flight of the Navigator*, or *Close Encounters of the 3rd Kind* instilled a desire to work toward mutually beneficial and peaceful contact with our neighbors?

Spend some time thinking or meditating about your core beliefs in this area and especially considering what you may have to work on and change if you wish to have peaceful contact.

AVIATION VS. MYSTICISM

As I progressed in my aviation career, it was made apparent to me by some of my "friends" that exploration of the paranormal, either UFOs or Mystical Studies, would impede my aviation career progression. While I still read the occasional book on the subject, I kind of put it all on the back burner for a while. I got a job as a flight instructor for Sierra Academy in Oakland, California. My new wife Terry quickly got bored sitting around the apartment, so she signed up for the Aircraft Mechanics School at the College of Alameda. I was about to learn that whenever this gal took on a challenge like that, she went after it with uncommon passion.

When Terry finished the first year of her school, she got a part-time job doing morning post-flight inspections for one of the local airfreight operators. As she was finishing up the second year and the full A&P (Airframe and Power Plant mechanic certification), the chief mechanic from the Beechcraft dealer in Hayward came up to the school saying he needed another mechanic and asked the instructors who was their best student. They pointed at Terry, to which he replied "A GIRL!" The instructors held their ground, saying, "You asked who the best mechanic in the class was," and so she got an interview and a job. Such is the woman I married.

Working out of the Oakland Airport for several years, we occasionally drove past the Rosicrucian Order buildings and their magnificent Egyptian Museum in San Jose, California. We wondered what it was all about, but never stopped in. This was the time a number of cults were active in the area, and I just didn't know what was what. We didn't want to get sucked into some cult that sounded good at first, and then pulled you in deeper and deeper. Besides, it would not mix well with my professional career. Again, I put mystical inquiry on the back burner due to career and peer pressures, but I still had this strange longing for answers that never went away.

One advantage of working at Sierra Academy was that we taught primarily foreign flight students, and I had the opportunity to work with young adults from all over the world. To the best of my recollection, I had students from Japan, France, Norway, Nigeria, Iraq, Iran, Libya, Brazil, and Greece. I'm sure there are a few others I am forgetting after over 30 years, but the experience taught me several important lessons. We had to overcome language barriers, and I learned to supplement the students' English proficiency with drawings and hand gestures. This probably gave me a better appreciation of communication skills across cultures than I would have received in a more "normal" setting. It also rapidly became apparent to me that people from all over the world were much more alike than different, and any stereotypes I had simply melted away. I made good friends with young adults from around the world, and the world got a little smaller and less foreign in the process.

After my stint at Sierra Academy, we moved back to Nampa, Idaho to be closer to our families and for me to take a job as Chief Pilot at a small flight operation called Clarks Air Service. I was Chief Pilot, Chief Flight Instructor, weekend airport manager, and assistant fuel boy. I said it was small! After a short while, I built the business up enough to hire another pilot, Jim Evans, and managed to keep the two of us pretty busy. I have fond memories of one winter weekend blizzard where we had 18 inches of snow on the runways and taxiways. The city snowplows were busy clearing the city streets first, so with no hope of opening that day I called the airport closed. We slogged our way to the grocery store to get fixings for Chili Rellenos and Margaritas, and then we had a blizzard party with Jim and his girlfriend (now wife) Donna.

Well, the chilies were supposed to be mild, but once we started in on them it became apparent we had some hot ones. The margaritas were not putting out the fire, so the rallying cry became "Come on Ice Cream," which cooled the heat a bit that evening. However, the next morning all of us noticed a peculiar aftereffect; these chilies were hot on the way out also, so once again the rallying cry at our respective houses became, "Come on Ice Cream!" To this day when we see Jim and Donna, the inside joke is "Come on Ice Cream."

While working at Clarks Air Service, I got hired twice by a new turboprop commuter airline in Boise, and never got to fly for them. When I dropped in a couple weeks after getting hired to check on my class date, everyone in the office was new. I asked about my class date, and they said to submit a résumé and application. But I had already been hired! Well, they had thrown out everything the previous manager had done and started fresh, but hadn't even bothered to notify us of the changes. So I went through the process again, got hired again, and then the company went bankrupt and folded before I ever started class. Such is aviation.

Not able to consider starting a family on Flight Instructor wages, I applied to the FAA for some Air Traffic Controller openings and took the Civil Service exam. Shortly after taking the exam, I was offered a job at Seattle Center[11]. I really would have preferred a smaller tower like Boise, but they were not offering that and basically told me to take it or leave it. So I went for a couple of months of training at the FAA's Air Traffic Controller School in Oklahoma City[12].

The FAA had some really good material on Theory of Instruction that we had to study for the Flight Instructor ratings, so I was looking forward to some quality instruction at the school. On Day One of controller school they packed the class into the auditorium and said, "Look Left, look Right, one of the three of you won't be here at the end of this course, and another one of you will not finish checkout at your facility." Not exactly the positive reinforcement I had expected! So began over two months of drinking from a fire hose with intense pressure to keep up or wash out. I don't think military Officer Candidate School is much worse.

I did well enough to get to move on to advanced training at the Seattle Center, and drove home to pack and head to Seattle. We found an apartment right next to the Center in Auburn that was kind of a new hire controller ghetto. I could walk to work, and there was a Piggly Wiggly grocery store right across the street, so it was nice in that respect. I was soon to find that the pressure cooker had just started. There were still a lot of hard feelings about the Air Traffic Controller strike of a couple years prior. I was from a small town in Eastern Oregon and didn't understand a lot about labor issues, but I was in for a quick education on that also. As I learned the issues, I believe the controllers were right to go on strike, and I believe Reagan's actions at that time set the stage for the decline of labor in this country that continues to this day. That December while I was still up to my ears in training at the facility, my wife surprised me with news that she was pregnant. It was nice to have insurance and a decent pay check, but I was certainly not out of the woods yet, and this put a *little* extra pressure on me to succeed.

Well, the old controllers were trying to make a point by washing out as many of the new hires as possible. It only took one little mistake and

---

[11] Seattle Center is an Air Route Traffic Control Center (ARTCC) which controls IFR traffic enroute between airports.

[12] Since that time, the FAA has outsourced Air Traffic Controller training, mostly to community colleges.

you were done. They pushed us so hard that I always felt a few days behind, and one day while working a non-radar separation problem on simulated traffic (using only paper strips and verbal position reports), I made the mistake of trying to be nice to a pseudo pilot and keep him moving, and in the process forgot to restate a crossing restriction that was already well behind him. That was it; they washed me out of the Center School for that one mistake, and told me I would be offered a job in a Flight Service Station. Out of 20 of us that started, they washed out about six at Oklahoma City, and all but three of my remaining classmates at Seattle. There was even a Congressional investigation into the high washout rate at Seattle Center, but I was just glad to be out of that pressure cooker.

Well, at the exit interview with our Center Chief (we called her Robot Woman because she was so cold and ruthless) I was told to not do anything and they would find an FAA Flight Service Facility for me. Well, some facilities are nicer than others, and some places nicer to live in than others, so I took a couple of vacation days alongside my weekend and we went driving. I had grown up in the Pacific Northwest, so I really preferred to stay in that general area. We visited Wenatchee, Ephrata, Walla Walla, Baker and Boise. The Chief in Wenatchee had an opening and really liked me. He also served as the Chief of the Ephrata Flight Service Station with a supervisor in Ephrata working that facility for him. The next day he was going to Seattle for a Regional meeting, and while there he requested me for the slot that was open in Ephrata. My understanding is that he saw them pull my folder out of the Rock Springs, Wyoming stack and put it in for the one opening in Ephrata. THANK YOU, THANK YOU!

One of my friends wound up going to Rock Springs, and I don't think he ever forgave me for that. Winters were cold, the wind blows mercilessly, and it is an Oil and Coal town with a bunch of roughnecks and reportedly a fair sized organized crime contingent. The Rock Springs Flight Service Chief at that time understandably had trouble getting good people, so if you did a good job he gave you a poor performance review and thus you couldn't get a promotion. The only way to escape was to be a screwup, so he wanted to get rid of you, and he would then give you a glowing performance review and help you get that promotion. There is something inherently wrong with that system!

Ephrata, Washington FSS was actually a lot of fun. The supervisor Jack Perrizo was pretty laid back and easy to get along with. He told us to use our best judgment and he would back us to the hilt. We still operated as much by the book as possible, but by allowing a little common sense it tempered the idiocracy of higher FAA administration. This was also nice since a good part of the day we were working alone with just a single controller on duty, and sometimes it would get rather busy.

Jack and I were both interested in computers, and I had been playing with a Tandy Radio Shack Color Computer that you hooked to a TV for 40 nearly unreadable characters of text per line. It had 4K of onboard RAM, but 2K was used by the onboard Tandy Basic programming language. If you wanted to save a program, you had to hook it to a cassette tape recorder with a special cable. I actually made a useful program to help the new controllers learn the area (Memorize the map and all the fixes, including distances, radials, radio frequencies and such). While not FAA approved, the boss offered the new people the option of using my program to help them memorize everything, and they all did use it, cassette tape drive, TV screen and all.

Jack and I devised a plan to take some computer classes at Big Bend Community College in neighboring Moses Lake, Washington. He and I would look over the class schedule and decide which class we each wanted, as long as one of us took classes in the morning and one in the afternoon. Then we would trade shifts with each other out of the normal shift rotation, and in this way we were each able to make about 2/3 of our class days.

After taking the basics of Systems Analysis and IBM 360 Assembler, I suggested to the instructor that what the town really needed were some practical courses using the new IBM PC's that were just coming out for small businesses. I had spent $3000 for a Columbia PC clone running at 4.77 MHz, 128 K of RAM, and Dual 5 1/4" 360K floppy drives, and was teaching myself to use it. I suggested dBase and Pascal as programming languages, bought my own copies, and proceeded to teach myself faster than the class could keep up. I was working with the instructor on lesson plans, programming exercises, and such. While the class actually slowed me down, I was getting college credit for it, and teaching the professor helped me learn it that much better. So while I was at it, I also worked in a little time as a computer lab assistant at the college.

One of my major coups for the college was when I discovered they were spending several thousand dollars a month for dedicated phone lines to connect their dumb terminals to the mainframe at Eastern Washington University over in Cheney, Washington. They were doing this so they could teach their one remaining mainframe class, IBM 360 Assembler. We had upgraded the computer lab from Apple II's (Very Slow) to IBM PC's, and so I did a little digging in the PC magazines (remember, this was pretty much pre-internet). It didn't take too long to find an IBM 360 Assembly Language Emulator that ran on the PC, so I showed that to the professor, and they ordered one to try it out. It worked well, so they bought enough copies to equip each machine in the lab with an IBM 360 Assembly Language emulator program, and then they cut the dedicated phone lines to the University in Cheney. I think they came out ahead in the first month. I just wish I had gotten a little bonus for that suggestion.

While in Ephrata I did get to do some flying. The Boeing Employees Soaring Club and the Evergreen Soaring Club would fly out of Ephrata in the springtime. I had already done some glider towing in Nampa, and wanted to get my glider ratings, so I asked the Boeing Employees Soaring Club if I could become a member. Fortunately, they had an exemption for a very limited number of non-Boeing employee members if they would be an asset to the club. I was planning to teach and tow, so I was in. I got checked out to tow gliders for them in the 180 hp Super Cubs, and then got some advanced sailplane training and took my Glider Commercial and Glider CFI[13] check rides both in one day. I was teaching in the club right away. My son had his first airplane ride in the back of the Blanik Sailplane when he was one year old.

There is something about flying sailplanes that forces you to focus and work with nature, not against it. You are up there without an engine, dependent on finding and utilizing rising air in order to stay aloft. If not attuned to the subtleties of nature and the winds, you may land out (off airport) and have a chance to renew your acquaintance with Mother Nature while you wait for your retrieval crew to arrive. Then it is traditionally incumbent upon you to buy them all dinner in exchange for their troubles. I only landed out twice.

The first time I was taking my daughter for a ride and while being towed to the normal release area I saw the tow plane rise, and a few moments later I hit the same updraft. It seemed like a large strong thermal and my instruments were showing a strong climb, so I cut loose early and tried to climb over the North end of Ephrata. Well, while the variometer[14] was squawking at me and showing a strong climb, my altimeter was showing that I was in fact losing altitude. This was not a good sign. While I might have been able to just stretch it back to the airport or at least the roads in the abandoned base housing area to the

---

[13] Certified Flight Instructor.

[14] A very sensitive vertical speed indicator.

west of the field, if I encountered sink on the way I might wind up confronted with power lines or a less than desirable place to land. Weighing the risks, I decided that unless I could manage to get another few hundred feet of altitude to insure a safe return to the airport, I would put it into an open field next to DK's Drive-In Restaurant at the north end of town.

The climb just wasn't happening, especially with what was now proving to be a faulty variometer, so I made a radio call back to the field to alert them to hook up the trailer, and proceeded to set up a landing approach to the open field. It was plenty big, but uncultivated and covered in weeds, so I couldn't necessarily see all the gopher holes or ruts. I chose the best looking area, touched down, and applied moderately heavy breaking to minimize the ground roll and the chance of hitting a hidden obstruction. My daughter, about 3 at the time, piped up from the back seat: "Boy, that sure was a short ride, Dad!" Maybe I was a bit embarrassed about falling out of the sky, but there seemed to be a bit of sarcasm in her voice even at that age. I bought the retrieval crew burgers at DK's after we got the sailplane disassembled and loaded on the trailer. Thanks, guys.

The second time was when I was trying to fly a 500 kilometer triangle course for a Soaring Society of America Gold distance badge. The weather was not perfect, but I had planned the attempt and rented the Astir CS fiberglass ship for the day, so I figured I would give it a try anyway. The best route appeared to be from Ephrata, WA North Northwest to Waterville, WA, then to Coeur d'Alene, Idaho and back to Ephrata. Both Waterville and Coeur d'Alene were surrounded by lots of green farm fields and thus were sinkholes. I would also have to work my way around the Spokane International Airport and Fairchild Air Force Base traffic areas, but the lift in the central basin looked like it was going to be relatively flat. My best chance of making distance was along the north edge of the central basin where the lava flows started to rise up into the low mountains of Northern Washington.

Waterville was indeed a sink hole, but I managed enough altitude to dive in, get my turn point photo, and back out to good lift. Flying along the top of the Central Basin was going quite well and I was making good time. About mid-way across the top of the Central Basin and a little east of Grand Coulee Dam, I noticed the smoke from a grass fire to my south that was going up to about 4000 feet above the ground, and then running into an inversion layer and just flattening out. This is not a good sign. It meant that the top of thermal lift in that area was pretty low. I thought about giving up and heading for home, but then I would never know if I could have made it, so I kept going. I worked my way around the north side of Spokane up near Dear Park, got a lot of altitude over the hills, and made a turn around the Coeur d'Alene airport and came right back out the same way.

With the lift getting weaker and the sun getting lower, I was running out of time. No longer able to maintain enough altitude to safely cross the lava fields and glide to a safe landing area, I started working my way down along the general route of Highway 28, getting some Zero Sink along the dry creek beds between the farm fields. I had hoped to make it to Odessa where a tow plane could pick me up, but wound up having to land in a fallow wheat field near Lamona, WA. A lot of the family farms out there have been bought up by the large corporate farms and the houses are abandoned, so I kept looking until I found a field near a house with a green yard and garden and a clean car. I tried to put it relatively close to the road but also had to dodge power lines, so I wound up about 50 yards from the gate to the road. The dirt was so soft that I only "Rolled" about a hundred feet, and when I got out, the dust rolled up over my ankles as I walked out of the field. I borrowed a phone at the farm house and called for my wife to hitch up the sailplane trailer and come get me. I made about 430 kilometers of the 500 I had intended, and was aloft for seven and a half hours. Not too bad without an engine!

When they closed the FAA Flight Service facility in Ephrata[15], we transferred to Spokane. The entry briefing by the facility chief there was

---

[15] The FAA later outsourced the Flight Service Station functions to private contractors, who continue to "Consolidate" facilities. In my opinion, there was a lot of benefit to having the pilot weather briefers living in the area where they did most of their briefings. It takes a year or two to become familiar with the local weather patterns, and having local knowledge of the weather, pilots, and flight operations helped you do a better job. Now the pilot weather briefers are in huge mega-facilities, behind locked security doors, in buildings without windows, and briefing you based entirely on the information they get off their computer systems. They wouldn't see a tornado or hailstorm right outside unless it was on their computers. It may be more cost effective, but I don't think it delivers the same kind of personal service as when the pilots would walk into our facility, look at the maps, and discuss their flight over the counter. In fact, I have more recently received weather briefings from people who were half way across the country and didn't know any of the fixes I was listing for my route.

very different, and consisted mostly of "Just follow the Rule Book and don't get ME in trouble!" He only had a few years until retirement, had feathered his nest, and did not want any waves at his facility. While it was his right to run the facility totally by the book, it was certainly a lot less fun than Ephrata had been.

In Spokane I was able to do a little instructing at a local club and then picked up a midnight airfreight run in a Cessna 401 medium twin. I managed to work a couple nights a week flying the airfreight, which consisted mostly of canceled checks[16], while working a full time rotating shift at the FAA, but at least I was keeping my skills up. In fact, a fair skill set was needed just to stay alive at that job. When the plane was delivered, the boss noticed me cringe looking at all the patches on the leading edge de-ice boots. These are like a very heavy duty rubber inner tube with chambers like an air mattress. When you encounter ice, you let it build up at least ¼" to ½" thick, and then inflate the de-ice boots, which cracks the ice to be blown away in the wind[17]. Modern Jet Airliners generally use hot compressed air from the engines to heat the leading edges of the wing and prevent ice from accumulating, and that system works much better.

Well, the first time I encountered serious ice with this airplane was descending down the west side of the Cascade Mountains into Seattle. This area is known as an Ice Factory, since the moisture laden air from over the Puget Sound is lifted up by the Cascade Mountains, cools, and is turned into a thick fog of super-cooled moisture droplets. I followed the recommended protocol, letting the ice build up to at least ¼ inch thick. I waited until turning onto the approach about 5 miles out from the runway at Boeing Field and then activated the de-ice boots. All the ice flew off EXCEPT for the ice that had adhered to the patches, which were weather-checked rubber as opposed to the smooth rubber on the boots. I had about 30-40 little one inch diameter by one half inch high ice pucks all over the leading edges of my wings, totally messing up the smooth airflow needed to create lift. This was NOT good and could

---

[16] Up to 25-30 million worth on certain nights of the month, but they were all non-negotiable canceled checks. This is all done electronically now rather than physically transporting the canceled checks.

[17] More modern de-ice boot designs work better on thinner ice, and it is now recommended they be turned on at the first signs of ice accumulation.

result in a violent stall well above normal stall speed. I kept the speed up to about 140 MPH all the way down the approach, flew right down to the runway, and then started to slow a little until I could fly the airplane onto the fortunately very long runway at high speed. Needless to say, I wasn't too impressed with the patches on the de-ice boots.

On another run it was a bitterly cold night, 20 below zero with good visibility at the ground but a ceiling[18] of only 100 feet. The route went from Spokane, Washington to Walla Walla, Pasco, Yakama, Boeing Field, and back to Spokane. Well, we got the airplane de-iced, loaded, and warmed up a bit on the way out to the runway, but it was still cold even with my insulated flying suit. We got cleared for takeoff, and were in the soup almost immediately. Spokane tower then gave me a left turn towards Walla Walla. Well, I turned, but the Gyro Compass didn't. It was too cold and the thickened old grease on the worn gyro bearings just wasn't turning. I took a quick look at the second hand on the clock, set myself at a standard rate turn[19], calculated the number of degrees I needed to change heading, and at the appropriate time rolled the wings level. When the magnetic compass settled down, I was pretty close, and all I had to do was make a small 5 degree correction to be on the assigned heading. I had been complaining about the sluggish operation of that particular gyro (actually a Horizontal Situation Indicator or HSI) for some time, and after this incident I managed to talk the company into putting a basic standby gyro compass on the right panel as a backup instrument.

Midnight freight dog flying is in many ways similar to Alaska Bush flying; you are out there with marginal equipment and almost totally on your own. Since the autopilot was mostly inoperative (it would hold a heading but not an altitude or a course), the company graciously allowed me to take an unpaid copilot when the weather was really down. There

---

[18] The cloud ceiling is the height of the base of the clouds above the ground.

[19] A standard Rate turn is 3 degrees of heading per second indicated by a different kind of gyro instrument. Magnetic compasses are subject to all kinds of lead and lag errors as you turn or accelerate, and are only really useful as a crosscheck when in straight and level un-accelerated flight. Thus, in the event of a gyro compass failure if possible you go to a standard rate turn and calculate the number of degrees of heading you need to turn, divide by 3, and time your turn for that many seconds. After stabilized in straight and level flight you can cross check your magnetic compass to see if you need to make a final correction.

was never a shortage of local flight instructors wanting to get some multi-engine instrument time, and while I was not supposed to let them take-off or land the airplane due to insurance restrictions, I would generally let them have at least one of the easier approaches and landings on the route. It was just fair since they weren't getting paid. I was only getting $50 a night plus $10 *per diem* for 5 hours of flying.

Fast approaching 40 and figuring I was over the hill as far as the airlines were concerned, I started looking for something to fill that gaping philosophical hole in my life. I explored religion, but what I found just didn't quite fit the bill for me. I knew there was something bigger, but wasn't finding it in the regular places.

About this time I got the word that due to a change in the *interpretation* of the Conflict of Interest rules at the FAA. I would have to quit flying at my part time jobs if I wanted to continue working at the FAA. While I went out of my way to avoid even mentioning my outside flying on or off the job, and especially would not recommend one flight school over another even if someone asked, it seems that somewhere someone in the FAA was abusing the privilege. The flying was what gave meaning to life, and this policy just hurt me to the core.

I went home and called a friend at Executive Flight over in Wenatchee, one of the top two or three FBO flight operations in the state of Washington. He had just had a pilot quit, and could use me flying corporate turboprop operations for him. It was a pay cut, but telling a pilot he can't fly is like telling a sailor he can never go to sea again. Flying, like the sea, gets in your blood and stays there the rest of your life. While it was a significant pay cut, I talked it over with my wife, we swallowed hard, and I typed up a letter. When I went to work at the FAA Flight Service Station the next day, I handed the boss a letter and said that this should resolve the conflict! He opened it up, and his jaw hit the floor. It was Two Weeks' Notice to the FAA, a secure government job with a pension. He had expected me to quit flying and be a miserable government bureaucrat for the rest of my career.[20] I never was one to take security over happiness, and so began the next adventure in my life.

Finding a place to live in Wenatchee was difficult. Between a big gold mine that had just opened up and the aluminum plant spooling back to

---

[20] In hindsight, I would have still had a pension and would be retired by now if I had stayed with the FAA.

full production, all the median priced housing in Wenatchee had been taken already. There were some overpriced dumps or some bargains in the $150,000 and up range, which was out of my reach on approximately $25,000/yr. expected income. My wife and kids were still in Spokane trying to sell the house in a down market, and I was temporarily living in a studio apartment in Wenatchee. Things were looking a bit bleak, but we had resolved to make it work.

CHAPTER EXERCISE: CONFORMITY

Does your job or do your co-workers expect you to conform? Is there strong social pressure to avoid outside the box thinking, or is independent thinking and creativity encouraged? Do your co-workers talk about topics like yoga, meditation, UFOs, the possibility of Extraterrestrial life, mystical experiences, and such?

If you were to have a UFO sighting or an extraterrestrial contact experience, do you think you could talk about it with your co-workers, your spouse, or your religious or spiritual leaders? How would you go about starting that conversation?

Spend a little time this week thinking about that and how much it might constrict you from speaking your truth.

AIRLINE JOB AND
ANOTHER PAY CUT

One week after starting the Job in Wenatchee, and before I was able to get any new résumés out, I got a letter from one of the major airlines inviting me to an interview. The boss in Wenatchee was very understanding, and allowed me to work my schedule around the airline interviews while saving the expensive turboprop checkout until we knew if I would be staying. I flew the pants off some Piper Seneca's doing charter trips for them while the four-stage interview process ground on. Finally I was offered a job with the airline, with a note that they would contact me later with a class date.

My current employer needed to know approximately how long I would be around as I had some special qualifications to fly Forest Service people into the back country and to do fire patrol and airborne command post operations. If I was leaving soon, he would need to find and train someone else to handle that part of the contract for the coming summer. This was about the first of May, 1989. I called the airline and asked if they had a rough idea when my class date would be so that my current employer could plan accordingly, and they told me to expect a class date sometime around October. That night I headed out on a charter that got back about 2:00 AM.

The next morning at 7:30 my phone rang way too early, but it was the lady from the airline personnel office asking if I could be in class on May 19th. That was about 2 ½ weeks away, so I said YES! I'm sure that when I called on behalf of my current employer, they pulled my file out of the stack, and then set it on top. When someone else delayed their start date, they grabbed me off the top of the stack and called. It saved me over 600 seniority numbers as they were hiring about 100-120 pilots a month back then. Sometimes nice guys do finish first! The only downside was that they had a two tier pay system with a B-Scale wage for new hires[21]. This was going to be another pay cut with no real assurance that we would ever end the B-Scale. I think my starting pay was $15/flight hour (approximately 80 flight hours/Mo, do the math) as a flight Engineer on a Boeing 727. AARRGG! The things we do to fly!

CHAPTER EXERCISE: SPEAKING YOUR TRUTH

Think about how much you are willing to sacrifice for what you believe and know to be true. Will you take lower pay for more happiness, or are you a slave to your income? Are you willing to risk your job or your friendships in order to speak your truth about topics like UFOs and ETs, or would you just play it safe and keep your newfound truth to yourself?

---

[21] Why did management institute a B-Scale wage for new hires? Only partially to save money, but mostly to Divide and Conquer labor during contract negotiations. The more labor factions with their own independent self-interests they could create, the more advantage the management had at the next contract negotiations.

THE MYSTIC CONNECTION

Where is all this going? Actually it is coming full circle. My initial assignment with the airline was as a Boeing 727 Flight Engineer based in San Francisco. We had kept the house in Spokane and I commuted to San Francisco to work. During the first year I flew a few times with a really outside-the-box Captain. This guy was a real free spirit with a subtle wry sense of humor. He would shovel all kinds of crazy stuff at me, and I would just heap it right back at him. We got along famously, much to the bewilderment of the Co-Pilots. One day while flying between Yellowstone and Jackson Hole, he dared me to explain to the passengers how the Grand Tetons got their name. (Look it up yourself, something about some French explorers who had been on the road too long). I declined, since I was still on probation, and instead handed him the PA. He chickened out and gave the passengers the straight spiel instead, "Off to our left you can see Yellowstone Lake, and off to the right Jackson Lake and the Grand Tetons." If you have ever seen the movie *Space Invaders*, Captain Jack had to have been the character study for the Martian pilot Blaznee. He had that kind of personality.

On one layover the whole crew went across the street to dinner at a place called Gaylin's Ribs, and one of the Flight Attendants asked Jack about his ring. He said that it was a Rosicrucian Ring. My radar went right up, and as soon as I could get him alone I was pumping him for information about the Rosicrucian Order. Well, this sounded like what I had been searching for so long, and my interest was renewed. Later that month we had a Spokane layover, so we planned for my wife to meet us all for dinner. Jack brought along his girlfriend (now wife) and we talked about the Rosicrucian Order all evening. To make a long story short, Terry and I wound up joining and it has been a fascinating Mystical study ever since.

Why is the Rosicrucian Order important to the UFO story? Well, among other things they taught me to be very open-minded and to consider a multitude of different viewpoints on subjects that sometimes go against popular opinion. I also came full circle in another way. Since I was flying out of San Francisco, I often visited the Rosicrucian Park and the magnificent Egyptian Museum in San Jose that I had looked at from the outside and been drawn to all those years before. I was also reviving my interest in UFOs and even wanting to get involved in UFO/ET investigation and research. There was an awful lot of disinformation and just plain confusion going on in the field, so I really wanted to find out who was reputable.

One of the Rosicrucian members was also a member of MUFON (Mutual UFO Network) and he gave me some literature, but it just didn't feel quite right to me at the time, so I kept looking.

Several years later, after we had moved to Colorado, my wife noticed that a Dr. Steven Greer was going to be speaking on UFOs in my town the following week. I checked my schedule and found I could just make it if I got back from my trip on time. Bone tired from several days on the road, I dragged myself down to the evening lecture and in just an hour or so Dr. Greer tied together almost all the loose ends that I had been trying to put together for so many years[22]. Everything just suddenly fit, the "Why" became obvious, and I knew that this Dr. Greer was onto something! Right away I started making plans to attend the CSETI[23] **Ambassadors to the Universe** training that summer. I didn't know how I was going to do it as I had no summer vacation that year, but I finally just made the commitment, sent in my application, and trusted it would work out.

A flight manager I talked to about attending a week-long seminar (I didn't tell him what it was about) was helpful in getting me a trip drop without pay. I was then able to pick up another trip earlier in the month, and thus didn't even lose any pay to attend. It was an example of a mystical principle I knew about, and had confirmed for myself here and many times since. If you have a strong desire for something and make a commitment, the universe will come into alignment with that desire and work to manifest it for you. The specifics of this Creative Visualization technique were taught to me in my Rosicrucian Studies, and I was learning to use them.

---

[22] One clue as to the reason for all the secrecy and disinformation: UFOs don't go zipping around the universe burning Exxon Jet A, and if we had their energy and propulsion systems, we would no longer be dependent upon the fossil fuel industry.

[23] Center for the Study of Extraterrestrial Intelligence   www.cseti.org

CHAPTER EXERCISE: CREATIVE VISUALIZATION

Meditate on this concept. **Have you EVER obtained anything without visualizing it first?** The time between our desire and achieving that desire may be long enough that we don't often make the connection, but I think you will find it hard to name anything you have achieved or obtained that you did not first desire and visualize. We can enhance that concept if we use a process called Creative Visualization. Let's practice a bit. Start with a basic meditation to get you in the proper state of mind, clear and focused. The breathing exercise will work just fine. When you are settled in, visualize what you want to manifest in as much detail as possible. If, for example, you desire a new car, visualize it in color, see the details of the interior, smell that new car smell, feel yourself driving it, and allow yourself to get excited about how it will feel. Wash and wax the car in your imagination, and feel what it is like to bring out the deep luster of the new paint, and how smooth and slick it is when you polish it. Then, when you have experienced the car as deeply and with as many senses as possible, RELEASE it to the Cosmic (God, Creator, Universe, whatever feels best to you), and **KNOW that it already IS!**

Now you can go to work creating the means to acquire the car you just built in the etheric plane, and know that it is being manifest into the physical as you work to be able to acquire it. Know that when the time is right, it will all come together. Do not put too many stipulations on how it will manifest, saving $500 a month will work, but don't be so specific that you inadvertently rule out winning it in that sweepstakes contest.

Remember that you can use this same technique to manifest non-physical things that you want just like I did to manifest the time off to attend the Ambassador to the Universe training. Visualize yourself doing what you want to accomplish, KNOW that it will work, MAKE the commitment, and RELEASE it to the universe to happen.

Here is an example of how Creative Manifestation worked for one friend of mine. He had a nice little import pickup truck that was in very good mechanical condition, but the paint was getting rather faded and the clear coat was peeling. He couldn't afford to just take the truck to a paint shop to have it done, so using the principles above he visualized his pickup with a nice shiny new paint job. He visualized the color, the shine, how good it felt to wax and polish it, and he didn't set any expectations as to how the new paint job would come about. He just focused on the desired result and left it to the Cosmic to decide how to manifest his new paint job. On his way home from our meeting where he had practiced this exercise, he hit an icy patch and lost control on a snowy road, rolling the vehicle and lightly scratching the paint on five of the six sides (the tires pretty well protected the belly), but surprisingly it did very little body damage to the pickup. The insurance company bought him a new paint job on the whole vehicle, and all he had to do was clean out his shorts. While it is generally best to not set any limiting conditions on how something is to manifest, perhaps you might ask that it be accomplished without undue drama.

Kind of gives new meaning to the old phrase: "Be careful what you ask for."

The whole process is supposed to be speeding up as the Earth and her inhabitants rise to higher vibrations, so let's see what you can manifest. Just remember the Rosicrucian principle that it is OK to benefit yourself as long as it also benefits others or at the very least does not disadvantage anyone else in the process.

PARADIGM SHIFT

The afternoon after my first UFO sighting on that CSETI outing in 1999 we all got together to compare notes and listen to Dr. Greer talk about his findings over the prior 15 years or so. There were eighteen of us there that year, including several scientists and a university professor. The vast majority had seen the same thing I had, with those on the opposite side of the circle having the initial events happen behind them. I was getting some good confirmation and corroboration, and was finding that no other theory fit nearly as well as the obvious straightforward interpretation of what happened. Even with all the years of pondering and the month or so of pre-study before the training session, I was not quite as ready as I thought I would be, and I was still reeling a bit. I was also wondering if this kind of thing happened every night, but later found that this was a rather rare and exceptional event and it didn't even get this good at most trainings.

By about the third night I was starting to perceive what looked to be subtle energy forms, like thousands of tiny barely perceptible blue/white fireflies, but taking on the general form of a humanoid being. Dr. Greer had talked about the Crossing Point and how the craft and beings were able to phase shift into the invisible, or if they wanted they could bleed through just enough into the physical so that most of us could see them. It requires a soft focus type of looking, using more of your psychic sight or third eye. If you stared too hard, you would lose them. It works best if you are in a meditative state with a borderline consciousness rather than hard awake and firmly in the physical world. It also works better without glasses if your vision is good enough.

We have a policy at CSETI that we share whatever we perceive with the rest of the group, and listen without ridicule or judgment. That keeps the channels open and allows us to get confirmation of what is going on, especially when it is so strange that most people would normally be afraid to say anything. Sometimes we can put together seemingly strange bits and pieces and form a bigger picture of what is going on than what any one person can perceive. Some people are primarily visual, others are auditory, and others pick up primarily on emotions. When I asked if anyone else saw what I thought I was seeing, some didn't see anything, but a significant number of others were seeing or perceiving the same thing. Boy, now the old self-doubt machine was starting to kick in. Was this mass-delusion feeding off each other, or was something really going on? I was still lurching around off balance, trying to figure out what to think. I wanted to be open minded, though not gullible, but there was a lot of room in between to explore and I didn't know quite where or how to begin.

The next morning I had an appointment for a massage and healing session with one of the local healers out in Moffat. Many of the old timers in the group were doing it and recommended that I get an appointment if I could. I asked her to open up any energy blockages and try to help make my perceptions more accurate so that I could more easily see and perceive the subtle events that were going on around us. She also worked through some emotional blocks that might be getting in the way of my experiences. Donna and her daughter spent over two hours working on me. She had these magnificent huge crystal singing bowls in the room, and when they would play both at once the deep harmonics of the two tones would just vibrate every cell in my body. I could feel it all the way to the core of my being.

I don't know what she did, but that night I had one of the most profound experiences I've ever had in the field. An hour or two into the evening, I could quite plainly see a group of humanoid energy forms to the east side of our group. I watched them for a while as Dr. Greer talked, and finally when I got an opening I asked Steve if he was seeing what I was seeing. He replied rather matter-of-factly that he had been watching them for some time. **OK!** I hadn't said what I was seeing, but he knew.

At this time Dr. Greer had the group line up in a slight arc to the east of our circle and in front of the assembled forms. About 2/3 of the group could see them, but some were not in the right state of consciousness and could not see anything.

As we lined up there seemed to be one being in front of each of us, as if there was one of them assigned to work with each person in our group. I kind of felt sorry for mine, being assigned to work with someone as new and conflicted as I felt at the time. We were standing with our arms and hands extended slightly, palms up, projecting as non-threatening an appearance as possible. I was able, possibly due to that morning's tune-up, to perceive a fair amount of detail this time. The "Being" was standing about 5 feet in front of me, and stood about 5 feet tall. He (just a subtle perception, not definite) had a slightly pointed chin, but not the classic Grey type face. The nose and mouth were slightly smaller, but similar to ours, not just slits. The eyes were slightly bigger and almond shaped, more oriental but definitely not the big bug eye lenses[24] you sometimes see portrayed. The neck was about the size of my wrist, and the upper chest reminded me of a chimpanzee, lean and wiry but strong. Everything felt peaceful and there was nothing going on that felt threatening at all.

After a minute or so of observation, it occurred to me that we were supposed to be "Ambassadors to the Universe," so I should give that a try. I thought projected, like talking but not out loud, stating who I was and what we were trying to accomplish, namely citizen diplomacy and trying to develop some peaceful relations with our visitors. I then became receptive for the reply, expecting to hear some word or sentence in the middle of my head. Instead what I got were two very distinct, very powerful emotions. The first was **Unconditional Love**, like your puppy dog has for you or you have for your kids. Even if your kids screw up, you still love them and want them to succeed. It was this kind of impression that came along with that emotion. This was immediately followed by **Intense Gratitude,** which really caught me off balance. The moment I mentally said "Huh?" the impression came back that they were grateful that there was anyone on this dysfunctional planet who wanted peaceful relations with them when what they generally encountered was the covert military guys trying to shoot them down.

WOW! I was again undergoing a paradigm shift, and that night trying to go to sleep I was again reeling. Was this really real, or was I just deluding myself? Many others had similar experiences, so that was some confirmation. Also, the more I thought about it, the more I realized that the message had been in an entirely different form than what I expected, and the message itself was entirely unexpected, so it was unlikely that it was my subconscious sneaking up to the surface. The more I thought, analyzed, pondered, and meditated on it, the more convinced I became that it had been a real experience.

A little later in the week I experienced what felt like a conscious download or RAM Dump. Images spooled in faster than I could perceive them. My thought was, "Boy, I didn't get any of that on the way in, I'll

---

[24] Dr. Greer says his contacts tell him the big bug eye lenses are like a combination sun glass/night vision lens to allow them to see in a wide range of lighting conditions, and are not their actual eyes.

just have to trust that it will filter out as appropriate." It was a little like the *Star Trek* episode where they are watching time and history scroll by at an incredible rate, but even faster than that.

Again, the implications of what had apparently happened had rattled my paradigm and left me off balance, but I was beginning to enjoy this paradigm shift and all the implications it carried. The big problem was going to be how to go back home and especially back to work. How could the world ever be the same again? The answer to come was that it couldn't ever be "The Same" again! I should have known that, for as a famous quote stated: "A mind once expanded can never return to its original dimensions."[25] Returning to work was quite a decompression, especially since I wanted to share all these experiences with my co-workers. But there were obvious hazards to my career and my credibility if I spoke the truth about these experiences at the airline. This is both highly unfair and most likely deliberately contrived to keep people, especially pilots, quiet about the subject. That conflict probably hurt more and put me more off balance than the week in the desert had.

Well, by now I was hooked and had to learn more. That winter I went to another CSETI week down in Joshua Tree National Forest. We worked on Remote Viewing skills some more, and I was having some more success at it. One evening after the classroom sessions our assignment was to get together with our car groups and each of us was to bring an object in a box or bag. Then we would take turns trying to remote view each other's RV "Targets." I was not doing well, probably because every-one else had brought candy bars or bags of potato chips that they had just purchased. I just was not resonating with that as it had no real long term attachment with anyone.

I was getting a bit frustrated by the time we got to the last task, trying to remote view what was going to happen out in the field that night. This added the dimensions of time and distance to the exercise, but in the quantum realms that is really no obstacle at all. Having been frustrated all evening, it was obvious to me that I was trying too hard, and I finally just kind of gave up and relaxed with a big mental sigh. Instantaneously when I did that, a very vivid "View" came flooding in. It was very detailed and rich in color as opposed to most of the faint indistinct impressions I would generally get in practice sessions. It was so real it was like living the experience, and I just KNEW it was valid.

---

[25] Albert Einstein and also attributed to Oliver Wendel Holmes, Anne Hathaway, and others.

While the others in the group were talking about a blue-white craft late in the evening, I broke in "Real-time," saying that it would be a golden-orange craft low in the Southwest early in the evening, midway between the trail and the road. It would not come too close but would interact with our lights a bit, and that it would stick around for four or five minutes. I knew without a doubt this was a good Remote View; there was no uncertainty in my mind.

We had a "Professional" remote viewer in our car group from one of those expensive highly advertised schools. She had spent about a thousand dollars for basic training, another thousand for advanced, and was now paying for a private tutor. She had also been having a bit of an ego problem about us amateurs, and this really pushed her buttons. No big surprise to me that when we arrived on site that evening the event was already in progress. It unfolded almost exactly as I had "seen" and reported with only a couple of minor details that I missed, like some smaller lights appearing off to the side. Some of the members got some good video of it. You can even see at the end of the encounter where it fades out and then there is a flash just like when they jump to warp on the movies. Hmm, perhaps those Hollywood types know more than they are letting on. The next day our professional viewer had totally lost it, and she went home.

Later in that week we had one of the first and only negative experiences I have ever had in the field. There was a very cold evil feeling that came over all of us. It became apparent that we were being psychotronically attacked, most likely by humans working in a covert project that wanted to disrupt our work and scare people off. As we had been instructed to do when someone is trying to affect or especially to psychotronically "Abduct" us, we all went into a very deep level of meditation, focusing on the breathing, pausing between the breaths, and moving into that silence between the breaths to that state where we were at one with the universe, in touch with universal mind, and thus "EGO-LESS" and beyond fear. When the covert guys try to "Abduct" you, what they are doing is getting a hold of your ego, that by which you identify with yourself. If you can transcend ego and fear, they have nothing to grab ahold of, and you slip though their hands like water. It frustrates them mightily. After about an hour of this, we returned to normal consciousness, chilled to the bone (your heart rate and circulation slow while mediating), packed up, and went back to the hotel early.

The next afternoon in class we discussed what had happened, and formulated a plan on how to respond. The first impulse is to get mad and want to retaliate in some way, but understanding the mystical principles involved, we knew that fighting would only give the opposition energy. Instead, we planned a group meditation to try to uplift their thinking to a higher level. As the Buddha said: ***"Hatreds never cease by hatreds in this world. By love alone they cease. This is an ancient Law."*** This is one of our most powerful tools against oppressors, love them and lift them up to a higher level! Here is what we did, as recalled in a discourse I wrote for a Rosicrucian Convocation at the time.

CREATING AN EGREGORE

"Whenever 2 or more of you are gathered ..." is a phrase familiar to many, but how many of you know why that concept is important? It seems that whenever two or more minds work together on a particular project, the creative effect is not just doubled, but instead goes up at a much faster rate. I'm not sure if it is logarithmically, exponentially, or what, but it really doesn't matter. The important point is that as we add our conscious efforts together for a common cause, the effect we have is increased tremendously over that of individual efforts.

As a Mystical lodge and as an Order we work together frequently! In the process we create an Egregore, or thought form, which some describe as a conscious entity in its own right. We all contribute to the Egregore of our order by our thoughts and deeds. In addition, it can return the favor and help us to accomplish our desired goals. In this way we all benefit from the Egregore of the Order. It is filled with the wisdom of the ages, and benefits us in ways both subtle and profound. By simply asking to be enlightened relative to a certain problem, we can receive inspiration from the Master Within. This can be invaluable in allowing us to accomplish what we need and to live more rewarding lives. It is a benefit of membership in our order that is hard to quantify or even to describe, but is none the less very real.

The Egregore of our Order has been created over many centuries, and is very strong. In the course of our discussions on this topic I realized that I had helped to create a new Egregore just recently. While working with another group for the cause of universal peace and a better future, we were very aware that there were forces inspired by greed and lust for power that were very definitely working against us. Knowing that we would get nowhere and simply empower these forces by trying to push against them, I was pondering how a small group of 30 some people could create a force powerful enough to overcome these very powerful and entrenched interests. We needed to create a morphogenic field of sufficient strength to lead the world in a new direction. We needed that 100th monkey to push us over the top.

While meditating on this problem, I received an inspiration. Every Consciousness we added multiplied our effect, so if I could tap into millions or billions of minds, we could create an overwhelming force for change. I reached out to the Cosmic Consciousness, and through other conscious entities I thus contacted, put out the word to the universe about what our group was planning to try to accomplish that night. I then asked for all conscious, aware, moral beings on Earth and throughout the universe to join with us for that evening's meditation. When we arrived at the field site, I shared my inspiration with the group leader, and it was incorporated into the guided meditation that night. The effect of having all this help from around the universe was so powerful that the experience is hard to describe. We were all moved emotionally as we asked that the Hearts and Minds of those in power be uplifted and changed towards the light of universal love and cooperation. At the end of the meditation, we were all asked to be quiet and receptive for a couple of minutes and see what impressions we received. I was startled to "see" a choir singing the Hallelujah Chorus, not in a religious way, but simply as an expression of pure joy. As each phrase built in, it was joined by exponentially increasing numbers of choirs, until very rapidly they went from horizon to horizon and filled the entire sky. The sound was magnificent in its beauty and power, and this sound *"Created"* a Golden White light that encompassed the whole world.

The entire experience was quite overwhelmingly beautiful. No one in the group doubted that we had been noticed and that we had had an important effect for good and for the future of our planet. I think there were people in positions of power who woke up the next morning and didn't know what had hit them, but who started thinking in new and better ways.

One person with an inspiration can have tremendous effect! If joined by others, they can truly change the world! Join with me in creating a better world for our children, their children's children, and many thousands of generations to come.

The only limitations we have are those we place upon ourselves, so **THINK BIG** and **KNOW** that you can achieve **ANYTHING**. Make your New Year's resolution a **BIG** one, enlist your friends and fellow lodge members to join with you, and make it happen for a better world.

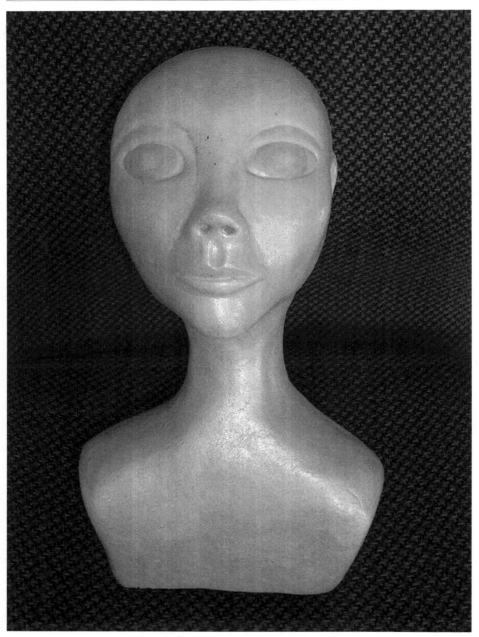

This bust was given to me by a friend as it closely resembled the energy form beings I saw in the Baca. These are reported to be a benevolent species working with us. They do have small ears in an indentation on the sides of the skull, not visible from straight ahead.

THE INTERPLANETARY COUNCIL

What is the Interplanetary Council? According to Dr. Greer, it is like a Giant United Nations, or maybe more accurately a Babylon 5, floating out in deep intergalactic space. It is supposed to serve many of the same functions as our United Nations, a forum for discussion between worlds, a place to find peaceful cooperative solutions, and a place to discuss and monitor emerging civilizations like our own. Dr. Greer led us there in a guided meditation and remote viewing exercise. I got some definite impressions and I felt I had made a connection with one of the diplomats who had an interest in Earth.

However, since it was a "Guided" meditation, the validity is slightly reduced, as you are susceptible to impressions and suggestions. So, to that end, I would like to propose an experiment. With minimal suggestion on my part, I would like to lead you to the Interplanetary Council in consciousness to remote view it and see what impressions you get. You can make a recording of your own voice speaking the words, or go to my web site and download or stream the Interplanetary Council meditation. Then see what impressions you get. Describe the outside of the craft, or it might even be a building on a planet, describe what you see inside, describe the impression of the council chambers, and describe your impressions of the diplomats you meet. This can include not only physical descriptions, but also emotions, sounds, even scents.

I would like you to do this now, before reading the rest of the book. Take notes of your impressions and save them.

Then, again at the end of the book I will ask you to repeat this exercise when you are perhaps more proficient at meditation and remote viewing, and again record your impressions. Send them to me at my web site to compile with all the other readers of this book. The object is to see if we get a pretty consistent consensus among a majority of you, which would lead to a pretty high validity of its reality and our impressions of it. If we are all over the map, then further study is indicated and the jury is still out. I can publish your impressions on the web site with your name removed. Once you have submitted your data, you can access that of others. In this way the data remains as pure as possible.

So, for the meditation, here is what you do.

CHAPTER EXERCISE: MEDITATION FOR INTERPLANETARY COUNCIL

Sit comfortably in a firm or lightly padded relatively upright chair, with your feet separated and your hands in your lap palms down. Take a series of at least seven slow, deep breaths, inhaling as slowly and deeply as possible, then pausing as long as you comfortably can, and then exhale slowly and deeply, and again pause as long as comfortable.

Continue, focusing on your breathing, until you are in a deeply relaxed state. Now, visualize your breath coming in through the top of your head (Like a Dolphin), flowing down through your entire body, and flowing out through the base of your spine and the soles of your feet when you exhale. Allow your breath to bring in pure love and compassion, and exhale any negative thoughts or emotions, in this way purifying yourself with each breath.

Now, start to focus on the pause between the breaths, and you will notice that in the pause there is a moment of Deep, Profound Silence. Gently go into that silence, and allow it to expand longer and longer with each breath, until eventually the silence will fill the entire breath. Become aware of awareness itself, not the stray sound that you may hear, but that by which you are able to hear that sound. In this way, sounds will not be a distraction, but simply an acknowledgement of your connection to the fundamental awareness that infuses every conscious aware entity in the universe. Then let the sound go, and return to focusing on communing with the deep profound silence that starts between the breaths, for this is your connection with the Cosmic Consciousness, the collective consciousness of the Universe itself.

Now imagine yourself as a Dolphin at play in the ocean, leaping and spinning and diving, just for the pure joy of it. Revel in the joy of your perceptions and your freedom. Dive deeply into that sea of pure consciousness, and then swim upward as fast as you can, leap into the air, and just keep going, faster and faster up through the atmosphere, past the moon, past our planets and out of our solar system. See the stars passing faster and faster, until you are out in intergalactic space looking at all the beautiful galaxies around you. Commune with the deep silence, and contemplate what a beautiful universe Creator has wrought. Understand how we are all connected through that creation and through our connection with Cosmic Consciousness, and how we are all thus "One" with each other!

Now, put out the intention that you wish to visit the Interplanetary Council, and allow your consciousness to take you in the proper direction. You can travel at the speed of consciousness, so you should arrive quite rapidly. As you approach, note your impressions of the craft or building. And now, ask permission to go inside. Most likely someone will guide you, or you may simply find yourself inside.

Greet any guides with respect and humility, explain that you are wishing to visit as a citizen representative of Earth, and ask if you may visit the council chambers. Enter with the same reverence as if you were attending a general assembly of the United Nations. You will most likely be ushered into the viewing gallery. From here, take in the look and feel of the chambers. How large is the room, what shape is it, how high is the ceiling, what are the walls like, and what materials does it appear to be made of? Is there a table or negotiation area, what does it look like? Are there any objects on the table or over it?

Now, pay particular attention to any of the diplomats that may be present. What impressions do you get of them? Take note of their physical appearance, and also any emotional impressions or telepathic messages or impressions you might receive. You might find that you make a connection with one of the diplomats. Offer your willingness to help with the evolution of humanity to the point where we can become full galactic citizens. Now become perceptive of what impressions you get in return.

Now, give your thanks and gratitude for being allowed to visit, and prepare to take your leave. Allow your consciousness to move back outside, and rapidly fly back to our galaxy, to our sun, to our earth, and back to your body. Your consciousness knows the way and will not get lost. And now, slowly and gently begin to return to normal waking consciousness, becoming gradually more awake with each breath.

While everything is fresh in your mind, make notes of your impressions, and put the notepad next to your bed. You will very likely find insights and inspirations flowing into your consciousness over the next several weeks, especially when in the hypnogogic state when just falling asleep or waking up, so having the notepad handy will allow you to take notes as any impressions come flowing in.

COMMUNICATION THROUGH INSPIRATION

Shortly after my ram dump experience, I was doing the initial line training with a pilot who had just upgraded to Captain at the airline, and he wanted to go out and celebrate his promotion. It was our only layover over 12 hours on the trip (to be legal to have a drink), so we got changed into civvies and at 10:30 PM headed down to the Riverwalk in San Antonio, looking for something that was still open. From the back of a little courtyard we heard some really bad singing, but that at least meant they were open. We headed into a little place called "Tequila Mockingbird" and discovered it was Mad Dog Monday, open mike night, and the locals were reading poetry and performing songs they had written. It was mostly a college crowd lamenting lost loves, but there were a few others in the group. Then a man, probably in his 40's, got up and read a poem titled *Star Child* that really touched me and triggered the latent poet in me that hadn't written anything since college. I started grabbing napkins and writing stanzas down as they flowed out of my consciousness.

As we were walking back to the hotel stanzas were still running through my head and I wanted to get to my room so I could write them all down before I forgot them. For most of the night I would get a thought for a stanza and have to roll over, turn on the light, and write it down, knowing that if I just tried to remember I would lose it by morning. In this way, from a spark of inspiration and a hypnologic state, the poem practically wrote itself that night. It was 70 percent done in the morning, and all I had to do was add a few more concepts that popped up later and polish the tempo and meter. I'm sure I had some help on this one, possibly connecting to cosmic source or my guides.

Here is how it came out.

FRIENDS IN HIGH PLACES

A bold New World awaits us
a spinning on this Earth,
an end to want and poverty
a time of happiness and mirth.

Abundant, free, non-polluting energy,
an end to hunger and disease,
the possibilities are endless
floating cars, if you please.

I have met with friends in high places
all this is possible you see,
It has already been given to us
and should be cause for much glee.

But there are those among us
who do not want these things to pass,
they would much rather
stick it to us in the Gas!

Our friends and neighbors we betray
their technology was given, stolen, taken,
all so these greedy people
huge profits could be makin.
(the relationship was adversely shaken)

Fossil fuels we keep on burning
our environment it is a cryin,
big money these people are making
while Mother Earth she is a dyin.

Minions of Darkness
have caused us this plight,
the only weapon we have
is to expose them to the light.

Legions of covert workers
will then march out from their cave,
humanity will have to grow up
and learn how to behave.

There is a new Golden Age a coming
of that we can be sure,
we are working very hard
so you can stand the cure.

The Angels are on our side
that I truly suspect,
future generations untold
our actions will effect!

The world will get a lot bigger
when we all realize,
we are not alone in this universe
and see it with new eyes.

If we fix our problems
and do this as we should,
we then will be invited
to join the cosmic neighborhood!

We have friends in high places
they want us to succeed,
it is most important for us humans
to persevere in this momentous Deed.

You can certainly help us
in our epic quest,
join and work with us
if you can stand the tests!

A New Universe awaits us
a chance to visit many places,
an opportunity to meet new "people"
with many different faces.

New cultures, peoples, places
a much bigger view of creation,
a future to look forward to
with hope and great elation.

I believe most of the concepts in this poem were given to me at a sub-conscious level during my previous contact experiences, both local and at a distance. You can probably see that in the message yourself. Perhaps this is another way that THEY communicate with us, through our intuition and inspiration.

CHAPTER EXERCISE: ONENESS

Using your favorite meditation technique, try to settle into the silence to where you are at one with the universe. Understand that ALL conscious aware beings in the Galaxy are awake and aware and able to perceive in the same way you are, sparked by the same seed of consciousness as you, and in that way are connected to you at that very basic level. Now, when you think you are at one with all, think of a person that annoys you for some reason. Understand that you and this person are part of the same whole, and contemplate why it is that this person annoys you. You will often find that it is because they are mirroring back some aspect of yourself that you don't like, and in this way can be a great lesson in that we can learn to improve ourselves in the process.

A word of warning is in order here. Part of the Mystical Path is Self-Discovery. This can be a bit hard on the psyche, or perhaps more accurately the Ego. We tend to see ourselves in a good light, and over-look our own faults. As we discover things about ourselves that we know we need to improve, it can become discouraging, daunting, or even depressing. In almost all mystical traditions this is called "The Dark Night of the Soul," that period where through honest introspection we see what is wrong with us but don't yet know how to go about improving it. The task of getting yourself from where you honestly find you are right now to where you want to be can seem rather overwhelming.

The task is now one of spiritual alchemy, refining the soul and casting off the dross of the old you. If you are having trouble coping with "The Dark Night," seek out a person or organization that can help you through it. Most any advanced mystic has already experienced the Dark Night of the Soul, and can encourage you to keep working on the process, and eventually, perhaps in a few weeks or a few months, you will see the light at the end of the tunnel. The end result will be worth it, I promise. You will like yourself more, and others will also find you nicer to be around. You will vibrate at a higher frequency, and since Like attracts Like, you will attract a higher level of people around you, or at least inspire those you work with to a higher way of being just by your example and the new light you give off.

So, now that you understand why that other person annoys you, THANK THEM for being a mirror into your own personality, and for the lessons they have taught you. Spend some time trying to learn to get along with this person and to resolve the issues that annoy you.

SIDE NOTE ON RAISING OUR VIBRATIONS

An interesting side note here: A number of years ago at one or our Rosicrucian Convocations, we were doing an experiment where the object was to sit in the candle lit sanctum of our temple opposite another member and try to project unconditional love to that person. I volunteered for the second or third round, and much to my chagrin the member who volunteered to participate with me was Dean, one of our older members. While Dean is a kind soul, at over 80 years of age he is also a bit crotchety and blunt; one thing Dean would do to dig at me was his habit of poking his finger in my International pilot belly and giving me a hard time about my weight. This was a sore point with me as with the jet lag of crossing 8-10 time zones a couple times a week, your body does not even know if it is hungry or not. Your body clock is so wiped out, you just eat when you think you should. Combine that with the bone-crushing fatigue and it is hard to get enough exercise to compensate, so I was having trouble with that weight issue and did not appreciate his jabs about it.

While I would have found it easier to project unconditional love to one of the other members, I acknowledged that the Cosmic had thrown me an extra challenge that night, and that if I could not get past my annoyance with Dean's playful taunts, how could I expect to greet our cosmic neighbors with unconditional love? Good one, Cosmic!

So we started the experiment and I worked hard on my Oneness meditation, understanding that we were part of the same Holographic Universe, sparked by the same Creator with the same spark of consciousness. I realize that the things about Dean that annoyed me were a window into my own self and perhaps were giving me a clue about things that I still needed to work on within myself.

Well, I did reach a point where I could project unconditional love to Dean as a fellow traveler on this Earth experience, and let the connection flow. I was in a pretty good state of bliss and therefore did not notice anything unusual about myself during the session. However, when we ended the experiment, one of the other members commented that she had just observed the most unusual phenomenon during that session.

After a few minutes she saw me surrounded by a violet colored haze or cloud, and an arm of that haze had reached out and encircled Dean. At that time she also noticed that I had become transparent and almost invisible.

Very interesting! Perhaps this can give us a clue as to what Dr. Greer calls the Crossing Point or what others call Dimensions or Higher Vibrations. As I raised my consciousness[26] up to a very high level of Unconditional Love and Oneness, my frequency became high enough that I started to appear transparent to observers. One analogy some have made is when you turn a fan on and the blades start to spin fast enough that you can no longer see the individual fan blades, they seem to disappear even though you "know" they are really still there. They say that as we raise our frequency high enough we become transparent or invisible to others who are not observing from the same level.

On other occasions I have even seen photos of other groups practicing similar meditations, and in the photographs you can see right through some of the people and even see objects behind and through them. If you are able to raise yourself up enough to become invisible, then you are probably well on your way to being able to meet our visitors half way, though don't think it is a prerequisite.

---

[26] Consciousness is considered by the Rosicrucians to be vibratory, operating on a very high frequency above sound, radio, and even the visible light spectrum. Just like the higher frequencies of Light are not limited to the speed of sound which vibrates at a much lower frequency, consciousness is not limited to the lower frequency speed of Light. Note how fast you can travel around the universe in your meditations.

WHY ALL THE SECRECY AND DENIAL?

Many people wonder, if the government were to find that there were Extraterrestrials, why would they not just tell us? The stock answer is that people would FREAK OUT! This is based in large part on an early Rand Corporation Study which concluded that if the citizens were informed that there was other life in the universe that they couldn't handle it, and there would be a rash of people jumping out of windows and such. Some of this may have been rationalization on their part to justify keeping the secret, as well as the power and control, to themselves.

There may be some types of people who would have more trouble with this revelation than others. I suspect that Scientists who have a lot of ego and reputation wrapped up in the world view they have been living and teaching all their lives might have some problems adapting. As a group they seem very resistant to change.

Religious Fundamentalists might also have trouble adapting, especially if they are firmly entrenched in the concept that we are the only intelligent life in the universe, that we are superior to all other life on Earth, and are the only beings created "in God's Image." It might be hard for them to accept that there are other peoples around the universe that are "equally" created in God's Image, and that their image may even appear physically quite different in many cases. The more anthropocentric the person's world view, the more difficulty they will likely have accepting our visitors as equals or even relatives.

Then there are the Religious Fundamentalists who in a way acknowledge UFOs, but perhaps as a means of control or out of superstitious fear tell their followers that UFOs are agents of the Devil. Those who buy into this mindset will have a huge amount of suspicion and take a long time to start to accept the possibility that our visitors might actually be here for the good of humanity. Consider their belief in the Evil Deceiver who sounds good and brings peace, but that peace then brings on

Armageddon. By this logic we need War in order to prevent Armageddon. Take a few moments and see if you can figure out a way to help these people get past that level of fear and suspicion. The whole "peace is bad" thing seems rather Orwellian to me, but it is also a very effective control mechanism.

From **DEEP SECRETS OF A UFO THINK TANK EXPOSED!** by **Anthony Bragalia**[27]

Regarding the Rand Corporation, it was originally started by people who had early knowledge of UFOs, and did a number of private studies for the Government and Military concerning the issue.

*You can find a lot of data on the Rand Corporation and Battelle Corporation by using the Google machine (or my favorite search engine **StartPage**, they don't log your IP address or your searches) and putting in **Rand Corporation UFO**. Happy researching.*

According to several reports I found, Rand's Executive Vice President is Michael D Rich. Mr. Rich is also Director of RAND National Security Research. His father was aviation genius Benjamin Rich. Ben Rich oversaw the ultra-secret Lockheed "Skunk Works" division where he spearheaded the development of the Stealth bomber. Rich Sr. is universally acknowledged as "the father of Stealth technology."

A friend of Ben Rich, John Andrews had written a letter to Ben Rich in which Andrews says, "I believe with certainty in manmade UFOs. I am tending to believe there are also extraterrestrial UFOs."

Rich in a *handwritten letter* replies to Andrews, "Yes, I am a believer in both categories." Before his own death, Andrews related that Rich went further in privately explaining that, "there are two types of UFOs, the ones we build and the ones 'they' build." *This next item is very telling as to the effects of the secrecy concerning all things UFO and ET.* Rich had told Andrews of his concern that the public should not

---

[27] http://ufocon.blogspot.com/2009/07/deep-secrets-of-ufo-think-tank-exposed.html

be told, but he said he had recently changed his mind on this. **Those "involved in dealing with the 'subject' could represent a bigger problem to citizens than knowledge of the visitors themselves."** [28]

Just before he died, Andrews says that Rich confirmed to him that "items" were recovered at the crash at Roswell in 1947. Rich also told associate John Goodall, "We have things at Area 51 that you and the best minds in the world won't even be able to conceive for the next 30-40 years."[29]

Another witness who testified for the Disclosure Project is Dan Morris. He was a retired Air Force career Master Sergeant who was involved in the extraterrestrial projects for many years. After leaving the Air Force, he was recruited into the super-secret National Reconnaissance Organization during which time he worked specifically on extraterrestrial-connected operations. He had a cosmic top-secret clearance (38 levels above top secret) which, he states to his knowledge, no U.S. president has ever held. In his testimony to the Disclosure Project and others he talks of assassinations committed by the NSA. He tells how our military deliberately caused the 1947 ET craft crashes near Roswell and captured one of the ETs, which they kept at Los Alamos for three years until he died. He talks about the intelligence teams that were charged with intimidating, discrediting, and even eliminating witnesses to ET/UFO events. He talks about Germany's re-engineering of UFOs, even prior to WWII. He talks about our current energy crisis *and the fact that we haven't needed fossil fuels since the 1940s, when free*

---

[28] President Eisenhower warned in his Farewell address about the dangers of the Unchecked Powers of the Military Industrial Complex. This secrecy and covert control of technology is what he was referring to. In fact, in his initial draft Eisenhower referred to it as the Military Congressional Industrial Complex, but he was forced to remove Congressional from the speech.

[29] Ben Rich attended a CSETI presentation shortly before his death, and after the meeting he introduced himself to some of the staff and presenters. He then made three rather astounding statements. 1. "There are no private conversations anywhere on Earth". 2. "We already have the means to travel among the stars, but these technologies are locked up in black projects and it would take an act of God to ever get them out to benefit humanity..." and 3. "Anything you can imagine we already know how to do." Gives one pause to ponder what kind of world we might have if the military mindset was not so prevalent.

energy technologies were developed, but that unfortunately these technologies have been kept from humanity. This is the real reason for the secrecy of the ET/UFO subject. "What the people in power right now don't want us to know is that this free energy is available to everybody." In conclusion, Dan warns against the weaponization of space and the shooting down of ET craft. This could force them to retaliate, and that would be our destruction."[30]

More from Dan Morris from the Disclosure Project Briefing Document and also available on the Website WantToKnow
http://www.wanttoknow.info/ufocover-up10pg#morris

US Air Force, NRO (National Reconnaissance Office), Master Sergeant Dan Morris

"Eisenhower wanted somebody to be in charge. The CIA was working primarily for itself. Most of the military intelligence directors were working for themselves....So, it was organized, but the name of the NRO was kept secret for years....The National Security Agency—the killers work in that" (agency). *"Secretary of Defense Forestall was the first powerful person that was eliminated because he was going to release information [on UFOs] and nobody has ever paid for that crime....."* *"Who was stationed at Roswell? The only nuclear bomb squadron in the world. We focused several powerful radars on the UFOs, and it caused two of them to crash. One of them had two aliens on it*[31]. One of them was wounded or hurt, the other was alive then, but before we could get him anywhere, he had passed on....I would interview people who claimed they had seen something, and try to convince them they hadn't, or that

---

[30] I was there at the National Press Club 2001 Disclosure Project presentations where I met Dan Morris personally and heard him say these same things. I can testify to the accuracy of the above report from personal experience. While my experience seems to indicate that our visitors would not retaliate and would simply move out of the way or even sacrifice themselves to avoid hurting us, I do not have anywhere close to the level of security clearance Dan did, so perhaps he knows of some instances where fighter aircraft were disabled or destroyed. My suspicion is that even in this case they would attempt to save the pilots.

[31] I recently met a nurse who was helping a friend. She says that her Mother was the nurse assigned to take care of the ET that survived the Roswell Crash, and she heard the stories when she was growing up.

they were hallucinating. If that didn't work, another team would give all the threats—threaten them and their family. They would be in charge of discrediting them, making them look foolish. Now, if that didn't work, there was another team that put an end to that problem, one way or another....UFOs are both extraterrestrial and manmade....Even back in Tesla's time, we had free energy. It's not that our government doesn't want us to know that there are other people on other planets. What they don't want us to know is that this free energy is available to everybody. That's the greatest secret. So secrecy about the UFOs is because of the energy issue. Some would like for us to believe that the aliens are our enemy now. There's no proof that I have ever read in any official document where—unless they were attacked—they ever shot. We don't have a threat from Russia anymore, but if we keep shooting at those aliens, we might have a threat from them. We should demand that our government stop trying to shoot down those aliens."[32]

I strongly agree with Dan Morris, in that ENERGY is the main reason for the secrecy. Even Nicola Tesla was squelched when he tried to give us Free Energy, because his boss, J.P. Morgan, could not figure out how to put a meter on it.

---

[32] I strongly recommend the Disclosure Project Video *Disclosure*. **www.disclosureproject.org** It gives a lot of insight into the reasons for the secrecy and offers suggestions for how to help promote the disclosure of the truth on these issues. Also included on this DVD is a PDF file of the 500 page congressional briefing document, with blueprint drawings of the Flux Liner, leaked classified documents, and numerous witness testimonies. This excerpt is from pages 358-366 of the Congressional Briefing Document, which EVERY member of the House and Senate received hand delivered to their offices in May of 2001. NONE had the courage to take action!

DISCLOSURE — OR AT LEAST A DARN GOOD TRY

On May 9th of 2001 we held the historic Disclosure Project National Press Club presentation in Washington, DC, which you can watch at **www.disclosureproject.org** or directly at **http://www.youtube.com/user/csetiweb#p/a/u/0/lkswXVmG4xM**

In fact, I suggest you take two hours right now and watch it so the rest of this chapter will make more sense to you. Download the file if possible, so you can more easily share it with friends.

Desperately wanting to participate in this event in any way I could, I could not work out my schedule to give me the days off to attend the entire event. I did manage to get a trip that got me home to Denver late Monday evening for about three hours sleep, giving me Tuesday to get back to Washington, DC, for the evening briefing and planning session. I had a trip that started from Denver on Saturday, the day of our all day public symposium. That would have made me leave Washington, DC, Friday afternoon to get back for work.

In another one of those synchronicities, the trip's first layover was in Washington, DC, and it even laid over at the same hotel Dr. Greer had chosen for the symposium. Since I was over the maximum scheduled flight hours for the month, the schedulers had to drop about 5 hours from my schedule to fix the problem. I called them up and asked if we could drop the first day of that trip, and I would pick it up on day two (Sunday) in Washington, DC. I told them they would not need to deadhead me to Washington, DC, as I would already be there and could just catch the scheduled van from the hotel with the co-pilot on Sunday. That worked great for the crew desk, and they made that adjustment. It was a Win-Win for both of us, with the only downside being that I had to lug my flight bag, uniform and clothes for about 8 days on the road, as well as my camera gear. I had to schlep all that stuff from plane to plane for three days while working my way home, but it was worth every bit of inconvenience to be able to participate in such a historic event.

The week in Washington, DC, was memorable in many ways. I met a number of the witnesses I had been hearing about for the prior two years. I got to know them as individuals, who just like me, had experiences they were tired of keeping secret. I chronicled the week in this paper I wrote at the time.

FIVE DAYS IN MAY

I finished flying a four-day trip May 7th at 11:26 P.M., drove home from the Denver airport to Evergreen, swapped my suitcase out, loaded an extra bag with camera gear, went horizontal for a couple of hours, and drove back to the airport to catch the 7:00 A.M. flight back to Washington, DC. Arriving around noon, I caught a ride down to the Washington, DC, Hilton & Towers on Connecticut Ave NW, where history was about to be made.

At 2:00 P.M. on Tuesday, **May 8, 2001**, we met with the 20 some witnesses to review their stories and get acquainted. Each individual witness was then taken into a separate room to consult with our Legal Counsel, Danny Sheehan, and condense their stories into approximately five minutes in length.

We broke for dinner at 6:30 P.M. and then returned for a staff meeting. We were all given assignments for the National Press Club press conference and general duties for the week. I was assigned to be the official Still Photographer for the whole event. We organized informal taxi-pool groups and arranged pick-up times to go to the National Press Club. Then we retired to our rooms to sleep, which was no problem since I had virtually no sleep the night before.

Day 2: Wed. May 9, 2001
We met, teamed up in cabs from the various hotels, and converged on the National Press Club at 7:30 A.M. (5:30 A.M. Denver time). We started setting up the room with sign-in tables and such. They talked about a Continental Breakfast, so I hadn't eaten beforehand, sleep being

more important than food. It turned out to be some small pastries and muffins, and coffee. I had to stake out a seat where I could get decent photos without a good telephoto, and things were filling up, so I grabbed an aisle seat on Row 3. The guy next to me publishes the Remote Viewing (Satellite photos) Newsletter from out of the National Press Club building, and has been to a lot of these press conferences. He looked over the witnesses, made some comment about them being all OLD GUYS, and that we weren't going to get any attention with them. He contended we needed currently active people, not retired. He also estimated that people would start filtering out after 10-15 minutes, and soon we would be talking to an empty room like at most press conferences he attended. I was still confident.

About this time our Press Club sponsor, Sarah McClendon, age 90, was wheeled into the room in her wheelchair by our logistics and transportation captain, Steven Bassett. Steve, who runs Paradigm Research (and later ran for US Congress on a Disclosure Platform), put aside some minor differences in philosophy and opinion to work with Dr. Steven Greer in a combined effort to get this disclosure done. He spent much of his time running witnesses to and from various airports. Thank you, Steven Bassett.

At 9:00 AM sharp, Jon Cypher opened the press conference. He is husband to witness Dr. Carol Rosin and known in his own right as Capt. Daniels on *Hill Street Blues* (that makes him almost a cousin, right?) as well as *Major Dad, Dawson's Creek*, and *Dynasty*. He began with a short statement and a few lines from "The Impossible Dream"[33] to introduce Dr. Greer.

Dr. Greer made a few opening remarks, and then introduced the first witness, John Callahan, former FAA Division Chief in charge of accidents and investigations. He described an incident where a UFO 3 to 4 times larger than a Boeing 747 paced a Japan Air Lines Cargoliner across Alaska for 31 minutes. He investigated and videotaped the re-creation of the radar and voice tapes being played back synchronized. At a meeting two days later, Reagan Science Advisors, CIA, FBI and unknowns listened to him brief them, asked all kinds of technical details about their radar, and acknowledged that it was a UFO. They then confiscated all the evidence, stating that the meeting didn't occur, the evidence didn't exist, and the event never happened. John was standing in the hall and did not get sworn into secrecy with the others. He also did not happen to tell them

---

[33] We made Jon promise to not sing at future events.

that they had the copies and he had all the original evidence up in his office. We now have that evidence with the Disclosure Project. The guy next to me started to pay attention.

Here is the list of witnesses that spoke that day. You can see their testimony though the Disclosure Project web site, www.disclosureproject.org

Steven M. Greer M.D.
John Callahan, former FAA Division Chief
Lt. Col. Charles Brown, USAF Retired
Michael Smith, US Air Force
Enrique Kolbeck, Senior Air Traffic Controller Mexico City Intl. Airport
Cmdr. Graham Bethune, US Navy Retired
Dan Willis, US Navy
Don Phillips, USAF/Lockheed Skunkworks (Corporate)
Robert Salas, USAF
Dwynne Arneson, USAF Retired
Harland Bentley, US Army
John Maynard, Defense Intelligence Agency Retired
Karl Wolfe, USAF
Donna Hare, former NASA contract employee
Larry Warren, USAF (RAF Bentwaters)
Major George Filer III, USAF Retired
Sgt. Clifford Stone, US Army Retired
Ted Loder, Professor
Major Sgt. Dan Morris, USAF Retired
Mark McCandlish, Aerospace Illustrator/witness
Daniel Sheehan, Esq. Legal Counsel and witness
Dr. Carol Rosin, Fairchild Industries/spokesperson for
    Wernher von Braun

You may recognize some of the names. George Filer writes the *Filer's Files* many of you see on the Internet, and is a regional director for MUFON. Daniel Sheehan was chief legal counsel for Karen Silkwood in her case against Kerr-McGee, the *New York Times* in the Pentagon Papers trial, Iran Contra, and others. Mark McCandlish is a world-class Aerospace Illustrator whose technical and aerospace drawings grace many magazine covers such as *Popular Science* and *Aviation Week*. A wide variety of people from many different walks of life, different organizations, and often different philosophies, came together to make this Disclosure presentation possible. All are to be saluted for their selfless dedication to the goals of this project.

As the press conference continued, some members of the press corps were observed standing, applauding and cheering. This is seldom seen, but what had **NEVER** been seen before was that the jaded, detached camera crews were also jumping up and applauding. That alone was historic! We heard that we had the largest turnout **EVER** at the National Press Club with the possible exception of when Ronald Reagan spoke there as a Sitting President. We had more cameras in the room than any-one could ever remember, and the Press Club staff answered more phone calls than they had ever received, asking for more details or contact info.

The staff asked us, "What were we doing in there?" Everyone was impressed with how professional and organized our staff was, and were blown away when they found out that it was all volunteer, and that we didn't even have a paid secretary. The guy next to me admitted that we definitely got the press corps attention, but that many reporters would be disappointed when their editors killed or hacked their stories to death. On that point he was correct.

After the press conference, some people had meetings on the hill, while many of the witnesses gave expanded interviews to members of the press, some of whom hung around for hours. As things were winding down, several of us took Sarah McClendon to lunch. She was quite impressed with what had just happened that day.

I had only one appointment with my representatives scheduled at that time, and it was with Sen. Ben Nighthorse Campbell's senior legislative assistant on Friday at 11 AM, so I went to work trying to get appointments with Wayne Allard and Tom Tancredo. These folks don't return calls, and only make appointments by FAX. I had e-mailed (they just get deleted), called, faxed as instructed, and followed up with calls. I finally secured an appointment with Rep. Tom Tancredo's staff for Thursday afternoon.

We were on our own for dinner, and I noticed a large group of witnesses that was gagging on the prices in the hotel restaurant menu, so I took them to City Lights of China, a Chinese restaurant I liked that was just down the street. After dinner we had a staff meeting at 9:00 PM where we were told that when we started the press conference 250,000 people were on line to watch the LiveCast. As soon as we started, we were electronically jammed. ConnectLive worked valiantly to reroute connections and work around the problem, and finally about 1-½ hours into the program they got the LiveCast working well again. (We know who did it, it was very sophisticated RF, not hacking).

ConnectLive put messages on their web site, and as soon as we finished, they immediately downloaded the tape onto the archives. At 9:00 PM there were still 13,000 people simultaneously watching the archived broadcast, tying up eight T-1 lines. We were sweeping Europe and Latin America and getting some spotty coverage here at home. CNN finally broke the story, and some others joined in. Most were reasonably balanced, but some were condescending or used weird up-your-nose close up camera angles to try to make Dr. Greer look strange. In spite of that, Steve said the response was beyond their wildest dreams, and that media experts estimated that over one billion people worldwide had seen our story. You may be wondering why you didn't see that much about us here at home in the USA. Many reporters were disappointed when their stories got killed at the higher editorial levels[34]. We pretty much proved that the Free Press isn't that free anymore.

Thursday, May 10th

We broke up into teams to hit the hill. Each team had a team leader and several witnesses. I was teamed up with leader Danny Sheehan and witnesses Larry Warren, John Callahan, and others. We kept reorganizing on the fly as new meetings were set up on short notice during the day. It was quite an experience spending the day with Danny Sheehan, discussing Constitutional law, philosophy, and much more. We had dinner at the Supreme Court Cafeteria (I called it the Supreme Food Court). Then we took a group photo in front of the steps of the Supreme Court. We were doing something very serious, but we were having a lot of fun in the process. While you are not taken seriously if you laugh in a congressman's office, we were sure snickering to ourselves about their reactions between briefings.

It was also very interesting to see the change in attitude of the congressional staff during the day. In the morning it was the glazed eyes /deer in the headlights look. While every single congressional office had all been given (hand delivered) briefing packages one to two weeks prior, no one took it seriously. After the Press Conference, they were rushing to get up to speed. (*Note:* This same briefing document that was given to every single congressional office is available along with the Disclosure DVD at http://www.disclosureproject.org/cd-dvd.shtml#2hourdvd)

My meeting was the last for our group that day and as we walked down the hall, team leader Danny Sheehan turned to me and said, "This is your Congressman, you run with this one." He soloed me 30 feet from

---

[34] *The Missing Times*—Terry Hansen

the door. In retrospect, this was very good timing, allowing me just enough time to get over the shock, but not enough time to get scared. By this time, news about us was getting around the hill, and they were treating us with polite respect. They were still trying to hand us off like a cosmic hot potato, but they did listen for about 20 minutes.

Thursday evening, we had a Closed Door VIP briefing, where the witnesses had a little more time to tell their stories. Sgt. Clifford Stone mustered his courage and gave a very emotional account of his first encounter with a Live ET. Sgt. Stone was recruited to be a member of an elite Nuclear, Biological and Chemical rapid response team. That was the cover story anyway, which allowed them to be called away from other duties at a moment's notice. Sgt. Clifford Stone was actually recruited for his empathic abilities, which he had had since he was just a boy. Shortly after entering the military and receiving his training, he was called out on an emergency response. On the way he was told that they had an Extraterrestrial Guest, and Clifford's services were needed to translate telepathically. However, when he met the ET, it told Sgt. Stone telepathically that it was a prisoner and added, **"I am afraid!"** At that moment, Sgt. Stone realized they were people just like us, with feelings and a soul. It also became apparent to him that WE were the barbarians in this situation.

Just turn the tables and imagine yourself being captive on a hostile foreign planet. You would be scared too. The ET told Sgt. Stone that his friends were waiting to try and rescue him, and all that he needed was to get out into an open area and they could pick him up. Clifford had great empathy for the being and understood that we were wrong in this situation. He developed an elaborate ruse to get the being outside the building and even managed some wire cutters for the barbed wire. Then he told everyone to go outside to see an amazing show in the sky. While they were distracted, he cut the wire and helped the ET into an open area where it was indeed picked up by his own kind. For this act he was seriously reprimanded and accused of "consorting with the enemy." His response was that he had been told the ET was a Guest. He was told to never do that again.

Over the years Sgt. Clifford Stone was called out on a number of "NBC" emergency calls, sometimes being on scene to help capture the beings on a downed craft. While not very common, they are brought down occasionally and they even have accidents or mechanical failure on occasion. Clifford found they are just as mortal as you and I, but also that the vast majority of them are here to help Humanity and the Planet. I for one can't wait until we can talk about that openly and face to face with our visitors in peaceful and respectful discourse.

We had some very powerful movers and shakers in the room for the Closed Door VIP Briefing, with names of attendees kept confidential. During the evening we made some very important allies among the guests. At this meeting I also met Astronomer Tom Van Flandern, Astronaut Dr. Brian O'Leary, and Jaime Mausson. It was quite a list of who's who.

Friday, May 11th

My team for the day was at scattered hotels, and I had an 11:00 AM appointment with Senator Ben Nighthorse Campbell's staff. We were planning to meet at the Senator's office, so I took the subway and walked to the Russell Senate office building. Since I was about 40 minutes early, and had not gotten a call back from Sen. Wayne Allard's office, I decided to drop by in person. Call it a live walk-in fax, if you will. As I went through the security screening, the guards greeted me, and asked how the Disclosure Project was going. They were really cheering us on, which was way cool. They knew who we were, and were on our side. I walked into Sen. Wayne Allard's office unannounced, and told the receptionist that I had been trying to get an appointment for two weeks. She looked at me, then at my Disclosure Project badge, and said "Oh! Just a moment." She called a legislative assistant, who came out looking at his watch. I told him I had an appointment with Ben Nighthorse Campbell at 11:00, and could give him 15 minutes now, or set a time for later in the day. He suggested 3:00 PM. I said we would be there.

My team that day was led by Jon Cypher, and included Ricky Butterfass, Karl Wolf, Carol Rosin and Bob Salas. The witnesses were running late from another meeting, so Jon, Ricky and I started. After about 10 minutes the rest of the team showed up, and we spent about 20-25 minutes with them. The staffer admitted a long-term personal interest in the subject and was impressed with our presentation.

We had lunch and walked around out by the fountains for a while. When the time came for my briefing with Sen. Wayne Allard's staff, the witnesses were detained elsewhere, so Jon Cypher, Ricky and I went in on our own. Not one, but three legislative assistants came out to greet us. As they walked us down to a meeting room at the end of the hall, I said that this must be important to get three of them to listen to us. He said, "Your issues cover such a broad spectrum that we all wanted to be here to cover all the bases. Take as long as you need to educate us, we are here to learn." Wow! What a change from the prior morning with the cosmic hot potato treatment. We spent probably 45 minutes with them, and they offered us strategy suggestions to best get our message heard. They were personally quite impressed and were working on how best to package the information to get the boss to take action.

(*Note*: after spending 45 minutes educating his staff on the issues and the evidence, I received a condescending form letter from the Senator, saying in effect, "Thank you for your interest in XYZ, if it ever comes up on the floor I will remember that you were interested." That is not acceptable in my book!)

As we walked out, we were trying to decide whether to go back to our hotels and get comfortable, or try to find something more to do. John said that Robert Salas had asked him to visit with his Senator Fred Thompson from Tennessee, since Jon and Fred were both actors. His office was right next door, so we just walked in unannounced. The receptionists looked at us, our Disclosure Project badges, and said quite cheerfully, "We know who you are!" The Senator had already left town for the weekend, so she went to get the scheduler to try to find a time for the next week. Out came a legislative assistant instead. She took us into a conference room and plopped down a stack of books, including the 493-page *Disclosure Project Congressional Briefing Document*[35]. Then she apologized for not having gotten through ALL of it yet. She had received the package the day before from another team, and had already made a good dent in the materials. We were impressed, and happily answered a few of her questions.

Finally, the day was over and we headed back to our hotels to get changed for dinner and staff meetings. Reports were coming in from all over the world, much of which was covering us far better than at home in the US! People were peacefully marching in the streets of England demanding the truth. PM Tony Blair discussed it favorably, and we were discussed on the floor of Parliament and the House of Commons. It would be just a bit of an embarrassment if they call our witnesses, swear them in, and have them testify under oath in England before our government gets its act together, wouldn't it? A review of events on the hill was encouraging, notes were made, and I retired to my room to write detailed reports of each of my meetings. I included who we met, who was there, what was discussed, what committees the representative is on, and suggested follow-up. These I turned in the next day for follow-up by senior Disclosure Project staff.

------

[35] The very same document you can obtain from the Disclosure Project at www.DisclosureProject.org

Saturday, May 12th

We met at the Hilton for the all-day public symposium. Approximately 300 people were in attendance, and with the long day witnesses had between 15 minutes to an hour each for expanded testimony. The crowd was captivated. We started at 8:00 AM and wound up at 10:00 PM.

After the symposium and the side discussions had died down, we recapped, hugged, and some of us gravitated up to the bar to discuss ideas. We didn't buy much because we were brainstorming a suitcase-sized electrogravitic (anti-gravity) demonstrator model. One of the witnesses, in an after-meeting discussion, had made the brash statement that for about $20,000 he could build a demonstrator model. One audience member in his group had said, "I will fund that!" "Are you sure?" "Yes, here is my credit card number, buy what you need." "But the interest will kill you!" "That is OK! Just do it!"

So here we were, putting together a shopping list and brainstorming how we were going to control this thing. With the high voltage we didn't think standard model airplane radio controls would work well, so we were discussing fiber optics. I suggested building it just a bit bigger so that a human could pilot it. (I just happen to know a pilot.) A C-band satellite dish was suggested, but on that scale we could not figure out how to get the pilot's buns more than a few inches away from very high voltage capacitors. While I'm through having kids, I was not sure I wanted to roast my *um...* derriere for science. We went back to remote control. Someone pointed out that it might be difficult to carry this into the halls of Congress, since it would have a large sphere in the middle, very high voltage circuits, and look a lot like a small nuclear device. Good Point! We will have to work on a suitable compromise location. Giddy from five of the most exciting days of my life and one margarita, I walked back across the street to my hotel to turn in. It was about 1:00 AM.

The next afternoon I picked up day two of my regularly scheduled trip, which as I said just happened to lay over at the same Washington, DC, Hilton. Isn't synchronicity a marvelous thing? The crew desk had graciously allowed me to drop the first day of my trip that started on May 12th. That allowed me to work the all-day Public Symposium on Saturday and then work my way home, and coming out with just the right amount of flying time for the month. It is a funny thing about this project, whenever I have stretched and made a commitment, things have just started to fall into place, allowing me to make the event, and usually not even lose any pay over it. Thank you to whomever is pulling those strings.

I was away from home basically from May 5th through May 14th, with only about four hours at home in the middle of one night, but I wouldn't trade the experience for the World. I sincerely hope we accomplished something important for all the generations to come.

As Paul Harvey is fond of saying: "Stand by for News!"

(*Note*: That news never really got past the "Former" intelligence agency operatives that are installed in high level editorial positions at all the major media in this country. See the reference to *The Missing Times* by Terry Hansen).

FOLLOWING UP

This note was sent to each congressional office we briefed in the week following the *Disclosure Project* National Press Club presentation of May 9, 2001. As you can probably figure, NONE of YOUR representatives had the courage to address this issue.

It is now up to YOU!

(No, don't look left or right, I mean **YOU! Just Look Inside!**)

Dear Sirs,

First let me thank you for the time and attention your staff paid me and other members of The Disclosure Project when we visited your Washington, DC, offices last week. I know your heads are spinning trying to assimilate all the new concepts and evidence you received. I have been working on this project for two years now, and I am still overwhelmed by the implications of the information. Rest assured, there is **much** more where that came from.

I hope you are being inundated by request from your constituents concerning the issues we have raised, and calling for hearings. In the interest of brevity, I will not get into technical or evidential discussions here, but simply try to reduce the issues to the most basic of terms, so you can see the forest through the trees.

Suppose you live in a tranquil neighborhood, and you notice someone new moving in. You go down to get acquainted, but as you enter his property, this new neighbor takes some pot shots at you with a gun. This causes you to retreat, and kind of destabilizes the neighborhood. Neighborhood meetings are called, but the situation escalates when this rogue neighbor starts lobbing rounds into your houses and property from his front porch. At this point, if not before, duly appointed law enforcement officers approach this person and try as peacefully as possible to take away the weapons he is using so irresponsibly. This is necessary to protect the others living in the neighborhood.

Now, step back a few million miles, and look at the Earth from the point of view of the Extraterrestrials. They see a lush blue-green planet thriving with life, including at least one sentient, conscious, self-aware species. There are many physical similarities, suggesting a possibility of some past genetic kinship. There is great anthropological interest in studying this planet and its development, but with as little interference as possible, very similar to Jane Goodall studying the behavior of chimpanzees in the wild.

All goes well for quite some time, but then the people of Earth enter a very dangerous period in their social and technological development. They start discovering and developing powerful new technologies at an ever-increasing rate, and turn these discoveries first to the development of better weapons. Unfortunately, throughout history we humans have learned to fear anyone who is different than us. Cave men battled other tribes over hunting grounds and different cultures through history competed for territory. More recently, leaders have used these cultural xenophobic tendencies prior to wars and conflicts in order to get us whipped up into a mindset where we would go out and kill the "enemy" without really understanding why. A fully informed citizenry would most often not play the role of Pawn in these kinds of power games, but our "Leaders" incite us to fear those who are of a different race, religion or culture than ourselves. This will soon be extended to trying to get us to fear what will be portrayed as the "Evil invading Aliens!"

Rogue elements on Earth that do not answer to Congress, the Joint Chiefs, or even the Commander in Chief, have in typical human fashion taken powerful new technologies, and using the brightest minds turned them into new weapons systems, new and better ways to kill each other. They argue that we must keep these technologies secret so the other side doesn't also acquire them, and thus the projects go deep covert and compartmentalized. War and fear of war keeps them employed, and so they promote that paradigm in subtle ways.

Clever minds figured out long ago that certain types of radar beams could disrupt the control and propulsion systems of these craft that were visiting, and a number of craft have been brought down. (This is the neighbor taking pot shots at you as you approach his house.) Some visitors have been captured, and may even at this time be held as prisoners without the protections of the Geneva Conventions or the assistance of the Red Cross. Imagine being held captive on a hostile planet and unable to even communicate with your own family! Not very polite of us, is it? (See Sgt. Clifford Stone and others for evidence.) But this local shoot-down capability wasn't good enough, so some of the peaceful technologies we have reverse engineered have been converted into very powerful directed energy and scalar electromagnetic weapons systems (Thomas E. Beardon http://www.cheniere.org).

This development could cause our neighbors to be concerned that we not only may not survive the dangerous post-nuclear era and destroy a precious and relatively rare ecosystem in the process, but are now developing the ability to reach out and lob pot shots into their backyard. It is approaching the time to call in the duly appointed law enforcement officers.

While this neighborhood meeting is going on, those innovative humans on Earth are making yet another disturbing move. Plans are being made for a Space Defense Initiative. This is to protect us from who and what? It won't protect us from a suitcase bomb, biological or chemical attack from within our own borders, or even 100% of "Rogue" missiles. Much of the very sophisticated sensing technology will be aimed out into space, not in toward Earth. It will be stated that it can protect us from Asteroids, and later they will play the last card of protecting us from "invading aliens!" The chemical fuel intercept missiles are not really needed since we already have the directed energy, particle beam, and scalar electromagnetic weapons to do the job once we identify the target. Some of these weapons have unlimited range and can focus on a planet in another solar system (T. E. Beardon). This is definitely destabilizing to the neighborhood, and may require action on their part. Let us call this **"Future One."**

There is a very limited amount of time for us to get our own act together before outside action is necessary. The disclosure project has assimilated a massive amount of evidence on the subject, and to a large extent knows where these covert USAP's (Unacknowledged Special Access Projects) are and who controls them. We have witnesses who were or still are working within many of these "unacknowledged projects." We know who has given orders to **down** Extraterrestrial Spacecraft, without consulting with the Joint Chiefs of Staff, the President, the Congress, or even the UN, and we can name names with evidence if called into hearings. This is a unilateral decision made in secrecy that has the potential to engage us in an interplanetary war that **they** don't want and we can't possibly win! We have many witnesses who are so disgusted with the way things have been managed that they are risking everything to come forward with us to straighten out our mess. Individuals have filled in various parts of the puzzle without even knowing what we have learned from others. We have a pretty good idea of what rings true by now. While it is possible that we have been misled or deliberately subjected to some disinformation, if only 75% of our evidence turns out to be accurate, we still have a **massive** case.

We, the staff and witnesses of the Disclosure Project, have made a decision that, knowing what we now know, we cannot live in good conscience without doing something about it. We have chosen to be **True Adults**, and stand toe to toe with the shadow government to resolve these issues. We feel that the path we are currently on is non-sustainable, and that the time is now to bring the **truth** and the new technologies out into the public sector for the benefit of mankind and the environment. We have taken responsibility for our own future, and the future we bequeath to our descendants. The walls are crumbling, and the time is NOW for action to restore the decisions and power to the rightful governments of our nation and our world.

We do not want to tear down whole industries, but instead would like to see them convert the vast majority of their resources to developing the peaceful exploration of space, and to solving the energy and environmental problems here on Earth. The energy industry has vast financial resources they can pour into rapidly developing replacement motor technologies for our cars, trucks, ships and planes. We believe that vastly more money can be made in these endeavors than by pursuing the path of conflict we are now on. (Some countries that depend primarily on a fossil fuel economy may need help making the transition, but this can be easily done.) As a bonus, this path gives us a survivable environment, provides unlimited clean energy to all parts of the world (thus eliminating the need for conflict and war over scarce and polluting energy), and gives us goals and hope for the future!

If we are able to return control of these issues to the Congress, Executive branch and legitimate Military leaders where it belongs, reign in the rogue elements, stop shooting at our neighbors when they come to visit, and start to convert the war industry into a space industry, then perhaps our neighbors will come by and introduce themselves. Perhaps they will even bring some of their toys to share with us. We stand to learn much about not only energy and propulsion systems, but medicine, science, ecology, culture, the arts and music, philosophy, and political systems as well! Travel is one of the greatest ways of expanding one's mind to different concepts and ideas, and Peaceful Contact opens up whole new vistas in that regard. We will undoubtedly find many new ideas to incorporate into our civilization to make this a better world.

Imagine the possibilities of **"Future Two!"**

The people of the Disclosure Project have taken a bold and courageous stand! We have proven that we are **True Adults**. We are laying everything on the line to provide a survivable future for our great grandkids.

There is just one question left: *Are there any **True Adults** walking the halls of Congress?*

At this point in history, we need a few of you to band together and determine the truth. We have taken the lead, and we stand point. All you need to do is use our cover and determine that there is enough evidence to warrant an investigation. The webcast numbers and video sales (check with Connect Live) of the NPC May 9, 2001 Press Conference alone should prove that the People want to know the truth, and are making an end run on the press to get it. Every witness I've talked to says it is like a great weight coming off their shoulders, and many have waited for this day for decades. Poll your constituents and find out for yourself. Then muster your courage, and help us create a future we will be proud to pass on to our descendants, a future full of hope and opportunity.

Working together, all things are possible!

Donald F. Daniels
Colorado, USA, Planet Earth, Milky Way Galaxy, Universe

CHAPTER EXERCISE: GETTING IT
OFF YOUR CHEST

When is the last time you got active and wrote your representatives? I'm sure there is some issue that is bugging you. It may be this issue of Disclosure, it may be health care, finance and banking, government corruption, foreign policy, or whatever issue is your passion. While you may think it makes no difference, especially if your representative is of an opposite opinion to you, it helps even in those cases just to let them know that you do not agree with them. They get most of their letters from those who think they can sway the representative a little bit on some issue, but it also helps to tell them you think they are on the wrong track. So pick an issue, and write ALL THREE of your representatives a personal note on the issue. Keep it succinct and to the point, and generally just a couple of paragraphs if you want it really read rather than skimmed. A personal note written from the heart carries 10-100 times the impact of a robo-form petition letter.

Now see, doesn't it feel better getting that off your chest!

TAKING THE SHOW ON THE ROAD

Even though we had huge coverage initially, we were shut down quite effectively in the major media the following day by the "coincidental" (and conveniently timed) discovery of 4000 documents the FBI "Just Happened" to forget to give to Timothy McVeigh's attorneys in the discovery phase of the Oklahoma City Bombings trial. It was one week before the scheduled execution of Timothy McVeigh, and the media spent hours debating the minutiae of the legal ramifications of this (did they need a new trial, would it delay the execution, and such), and thus one of the biggest stories in history got pushed right off the radar scope.

We had proven that the media was not "Free," and the decision was made to "Take the Disclosure Show on the Road." where we could make some inroads at the local level. A couple of weeks after the National Press Club event, I was called by the Disclosure Project, asking if I could be Major Domo for the initial Campaign for Disclosure World Tour event in the Denver area mid-June. I had to look up what a Major-Domo does, but accepted, and by "serendipity" I had vacation during the week prior, so I could devote sufficient time to setting up the event.

First, I had to find a venue, and we had no idea how many people would show up. We were also trying to present these meetings for free and were operating on a shoestring budget. The best I could find was the Chemistry Auditorium at the University of Colorado in Boulder. We got the room and projectionist for under $200. I started putting together a promotion campaign, again on a serious budget. I had a network of local CSETI working group members, and I put out the call for help. We designed a flyer, e-mailed it to the group, and asked each person to make 5-10 copies and post them in bookstores, grocery stores and libraries, anywhere they could get permission to post. Call it distributed publication, but it worked well. One member hooked me up with a Public Access TV Program in Boulder, and I found I was already scheduled for my first TV Interview (in my Life). This was stretching my comfort zone quite a bit, but the cause was worth whatever effort I could make. Throughout this whole process I was careful to not mention or allow the mention of the specific airline I worked for.

While in Boulder for the Interview, I checked details at the venue, and happened to see a bumper sticker that said something to the effect that "In these times of rampant Deceit, it was an act of extreme courage to Tell the Truth!" I made a note to use that in my Introduction of Dr. Greer.

Our real break in Promotion came the day before the event when one of my friends with media contacts called to tell me he had booked us on the *Reggie Rivers* show. It was the largest drive-time radio show in the Denver market at the time with an audience of about a million people. He gave me a phone number to call into the studio and informed me I was on the air in an hour. GULP! Since Dr. Greer was airborne at the time and due to land shortly after we started the radio program, I called another group member who lived close to the airport, asked her to run out there, check the business center for a quiet phone, and then go meet Dr. Greer at the gate as he got off the plane. (This was June 2001, pre-9/11). She then ushered him to a phone and he replaced me on the radio program about 45 minutes into the two-hour program. This allowed us to reach a huge audience.

The next morning in Boulder we arrived several hours early to set up and move books and videos into the building. People were already lining up. The auditorium had a listed capacity of 508 people, but they were crowding into the aisles, entryways, and even sitting on the floor in front. Some were lying on their backs behind the instructor's lab table, and looking straight up at the screen. Unfortunately, even at that, we had to turn several hundred people away as we simply could not physically get them in the room.

We had some well-organized detractors. There was a group there calling themselves "The Allies of Humanity," which was passing out flyers calling themselves the "Other" disclosure project. We made them move outside to distribute their literature, as we had rented the space inside. Researching their literature on the internet later, I found that it appeared to me to be very well done psychological disinformation, designed to create doubt and fear in people if open contact were to happen. It also appeared to be very carefully targeted at Dr. Greer, and indeed there was a web page almost hysterically trying to debunk our major points. They had done their research and had targeted us. Perhaps we were too close to the truth, and someone was worried. I simply made the disclaimer to the audience that they were an entirely different group and that we had different opinions on the issues. Later, as we started the Disclosure Video, a classic MIB (Man in Black) stood up and started screaming that we couldn't show that video. He then proceeded to beat on the door to the projection room, demanding to be let in. Fortunately, the door was locked and the projectionist did not open it. Our "Security" people in the back quietly escorted him out of the room. Again, this was a sign that we had the attention of some very powerful people.

You can order your own copy of the video at:
http://www.disclosureproject.org/cd-dvd.shtml#2hourdvd

or

http://www.disclosureproject.org/shop.htm#Disclosure Witness DVD

THE CONDON REPORT

I didn't realize until later that UC Boulder was the home of Dr. Condon, of *Condon Report* fame. Thirty-two years earlier Dr. Condon had issued this report:

SCIENTIFIC STUDY OF UNIDENTIFIED FLYING OBJECTS

Conducted by the University of Colorado
Under Research Contract Number 44620-67-C-0035
With the United States Air Force

Dr. Edward U. Condon, Scientific Director

[1968]

A description on the internet had this to say in summary about the report, commonly called the *Condon Report* and two other reports of the time:

For a period of four days in 1953, the Central Intelligence Agency convened a panel of scientific consultants to consider whether UFOs **constitute a threat to national defense**. *This panel included H.P. Robertson (chairman), Luis Alvarez, Lloyd Berkner, Samuel A. Goudsmit and Thornton Page; with Frederick C. Durant and J. Allen Hynek serving as associate members. The panel concluded that there was "no evidence that the phenomena indicate a need for the revision of current scientific concepts," and that "the evidence ... shows no indication that these phenomena constitute a direct physical threat to national security" (Jacobs, 1975).*

The Battelle Memorial Institute, under contract to the Air Force from 1951 to 1954, conducted the second study. It was primarily a statistical analysis of the conditions and characteristics of UFO reports, though it also provided scientific services and included transcripts of several notable sightings. The subsequent report was initially classified, though later released as "Blue Book Special Report No. 14" in 1955. It contains a wealth of information and arrives at the notable conclusion that the more complete the data and the better the report; the more likely it was that the report would remain unidentified (Jacobs, 1975).

On February 3, 1966, the Air Force convened an "Ad Hoc Committee to Review Project Blue Book." Its members included Brian O'Brien (chairman), Launor Carter, Jesse Orlansky, Richard Porter, Carl Sagan, and Willis A. Ware. The committee recommended that the Air Force negotiate contracts "with a few selected universities to provide selected teams to investigate promptly and in depth certain selected sightings of UFOs." This led eventually to the Air Force contract with the University of Colorado in October 1966. The project director was Professor Edward U. Condon, a very distinguished physicist and a man of strong and independent character. Work on this contract was carried out over a two-year period with a substantial scientific staff, resulting in the publication of the "Scientific Study of Unidentified Flying Objects" in January 1969.

Consequently, on December 17, 1969, Air Force Secretary Robert C. Seamans, Jr., announced the closure of Project Blue Book. Project Blue Book officially closed on Jan 30, 1970.

The main misconception was that the *Condon Report* said UFOs don't exist. What it really said is that *they present no threat to the national security*. It was still used effectively to close Project Blue Book and remove the government from the debate. This is just one example of carefully manipulating perceptions by implying one conclusion when the report actually said something quite different.

Thirty two years later we over-filled[36] the Chemistry Auditorium on this same UC Boulder campus, and while also stating that there was no threat to the national security, we also said there was very much of an interest in the UFO field. The synchronistic implications of our choice of venue to launch the Campaign for Disclosure had to make me laugh when I discovered them.

When I turned my team loose to creatively promote and run the event, one came up with an interesting idea. We had not found one Congressman or Senator with the guts to call for an investigation (The last was Congressman Gerald Ford in 1966), so one member of my team

---

[36] We had probably over 800 people in a 500 seat auditorium, sitting on the stairs of the aisles, on the floor up front, lying flat on their back behind the instructors table, and wedged in the entry coves. We unfortunately had to turn several hundred people away as there just physically wasn't any more room, and I was also worried about fire code.

pre-printed envelopes and a basic letter to the local Congressmen and Senators. She had pre-stamped envelopes ready, and members of the audience were invited after the show to pick up envelopes for their representatives, add a personal note, and she would mail them at her expense.

Several hundred letters went out that afternoon, yet the representatives insisted there was no demand by their constituents to open an investigation, and many stated that they had only received one or two letters. We know that we mailed hundreds that day alone, so something was wrong. Either the letters were being intercepted, or someone was dodging the issue. Perhaps they also got the hint when years earlier Congressman Schiff from New Mexico, Dr. Steven Greer, and his assistant Shari Adamiak, all three almost simultaneously developed full blown metastatic melanoma.

This was most unusual as it did not start as a carcinoma or have a defined point of origin. Dr. Greer was the only one of the three to survive. This was just as Congressman Schiff was preparing to hold congressional hearings on the UFO/ET issue. Many in Congress probably took this as a warning that if they approached the UFO/ET subject, they too would be targeted. That goes a long way toward explaining the Cosmic Hot Potato phenomenon we experienced after the Disclosure Conference in DC.

Shortly after the presentation, I was invited to speak to a breakfast meeting consisting of local mental health professionals and clergy. About this same time I was getting in trouble at work. I carried an "Official Star Fleet Identification Card" which is actually a Book and Record club card for *Star Trek, The Next Generation*. It was designed so that in your wallet credit card slot you could just see the Official Star Fleet Identification part, and it looked so good I just HAD to carry it. I had been showing it to a Flight Attendant who was a real Trekkie, and had rather flippantly said that I was Dual-Qualified.

We had a good laugh, but apparently the Co-Pilot had either never heard of *Star Trek* (is he from this planet?) or had no sense of humor. I received a call from the Chief Pilot, telling me that I had been removed from my next trip with pay (Polite for Grounded) and that I had to see the company doctor before I flew again. I asked what this was about, but he was rather evasive. Apparently complaints were coming in through our Corporate Headquarters, which was strange, since normally anything like that would come through the Domicile where I worked. It made me wonder if the MIB from our presentation was trying to pull the classic trashing of the reputation thing to silence me. It wouldn't be too hard for an intelligence operative to figure out who my employer was.

I didn't know exactly what the company doctor was going to ask or what all to prepare for, but I knew that it was basically a Psych-Eval. If they came in with prejudices or had been fed false information, I knew that it could trash my flying career and even my ability to hold a pilot's license to fly anything. It was not a pleasant time. I got my documentation together on some things I thought they might ask about, got letters from some of the scientists who were there when the Blue Spotlight event happened, and talked to my union reps, who were not all that sympathetic or helpful.

I went in to see the Doctor all by myself at the appointed time, not really knowing what to expect. Fortunately, the doctor was open minded and fair. He looked at the wallet card and said, "It says *Star Trek* right on it!" He asked a couple of questions to make sure I wouldn't do something stupid like roll the jet upside down if I saw a UFO, and proceeded to declare me perfectly sane.

Then, just as he was signing the form to return me to service, he asked about that Blue Spotlight. OH BOY, here we go! I told him that event had actually happened, here were letters from some of the scientists in the group who had witnessed it, and that the illogical thing to do would be to deny it. He looked at the letters, had to agree, and sent me upstairs with a letter saying I was "Certified Sane," a rather dubious distinction. The up side was that now I could talk about my experiences more openly. What could they do about it?

I was a bit ticked about the whole ordeal, and when showing the Chief Pilot my wallet card and the letter from the doctor, I realized that for just a moment I actually had the upper hand. I asked the Chief Pilot if I now had permission to talk about the subject of UFOs while on duty. While he suggested I choose my audience a bit more carefully, yes, I could talk about it with my fellow pilots. This may be a historic first from airline management, official permission to talk about UFOs.

While all this was going on, I was preparing my talk for the breakfast meeting with the psychologists and clergy[37]. I have to admit there was a bit of intimidation factor there, but the talk on *The Implications of Extraterrestrial Contact* was very well received. I had a whole room full of professionals who volunteered to support me if I had any more trouble at work. This helped me alleviate the remaining self-doubt from the

---

[37] Interestingly when I asked the clergy members if they had ever discussed the possibility of other life in the universe with their congregations, a surprising number had. Perhaps it was just Boulder, but it was encouraging.

whole episode. I still drop in with them for meetings of interest, and they still remember me and enjoy visiting and catching up on what is new.

Meanwhile, the Campaign for Disclosure World Tour was continuing in other cities around the country, and usually had packed auditoriums. Very little news coverage occurred outside of the smaller independent local media, and there was getting to be even less and less of that. Many small town newspapers have been bought up by the major news affiliates, and even they are now afraid to venture into "controversial" territory. We had tested the media system and found it to be tightly controlled, and there has been even more consolidation since. For a well-documented explanation of how this has been done, I recommend the book *The Missing Times* by Terry Hansen (www.xlibris.com) or more specifically http://www2.xlibris.com/bookstore/bookdisplay.asp?bookid=2313.

In the book Terry Hansen describes and documents the revolving door between the security agencies and high level editorial positions in the major media. "Former" NSA and other security operatives now occupy many high level editorial positions in our country's media organizations and this was done after the incident where a UFO shut down the guidance systems of multiple ICBM's in Montana (and we hear rumor that missiles were shut down in Russia at about the same time).

This incident was of great concern to some of our military leaders, although two of our witnesses, Dwynne Arneson and Robert Salas[38], who were at the National Press Club and were directly involved, did not feel it was a threatening event. They felt that "they" were simply telling us we shouldn't play that (nuclear war) game, and that they had the ability to shut us down and prevent it. The witnesses felt it was more of a "Fatherly Suggestion" than a threat to our national security. Perhaps some of our Military leaders felt threatened because they realized they weren't the biggest dog in the junkyard, and thus transferred their fear and inferiority onto the public. The excuse was that the American public would panic if they knew our missiles could be shut down, but I think most of us would be comforted knowing that someone with more brains and less ego could prevent the insanity of nuclear war on both sides. After that time, the Intelligence Agencies felt the need to more tightly control the media on such issues, and so it has become. As a side note,

---

[38] See *Faded Giant* by Robert Salas,
http://www.ufopop.org/Special/FadedGiant.htm

it was right after that event that US/Russian Détente started up in earnest. Perhaps our respective leaders took the hint from this gentle nudge.

If you want a short three-minute visual that illustrates this concept, and pretty well proves that most of the media talking heads get their script from the same puppet masters, check out this video of Conan O'Brian getting his revenge and proving that we have very little independent media left in this country.

http://www.youtube.com/watch?v=GME5nq_oSR4&feature=player_ embedded [39]

---

[39] Conan O'Brian's revenge:
http://www.youtube.com/watch?v=GME5nq_oSR4&feature=player_embedded

CHAPTER EXERCISE: TALKING ABOUT YOUR EXPERIENCES

Do you know anyone who has had a UFO or ET encounter? Perhaps you know more than one. Organize a get-together, preferably in person, but if not able, then by phone on a conference call.[40] Meeting in person is best as you can share the emotions of the experiences. Lay out some basic ground rules about confidentiality and that you will all respect each person's opinions and consider them with an open mind. There will be no ridicule, even if their high strangeness is beyond your experience. Many things that happen are so outside the box they may not make sense until a number of people share experiences and collectively build a bigger picture.

If you have had an encounter yourself, then I suggest you break the ice and demonstrate that it is a safe environment by sharing your experience(s) first. In this way others are more inclined to feel safe and open up to the group. You might be astounded at the stories you hear from others that you had no idea had occurred.[41] Keeping something like this inside really tears someone up, and is I think one of the greatest harms caused by the PsyOps Disinformation campaign. They deliberately teach the public though subtle example in films and TV to laugh at and ridicule anyone who tells such a story. Notice your own reactions as others share, and be conscious of that pre-programmed reaction in yourself. You may find you have some more work to do on yourself in this regard. Many times at these kinds of gatherings we have found that it is tremendously healing for those involved to be able to share their truth in a safe environment, often for the first time in their lives.

---

[40] You can set up conference calls on Skype, Google Talk, or Microsoft Messenger that are free if everyone is using their computer and just a couple cents a minute to add phones. You can also use one of the free conference call services like www.FreeConferenceCall.com, www.FreeConference.com, or www.GoToMeeting.com/Conference-Call where you generally only pay for your own toll call, but most cell phone plans are free on weekends, so have a blast.

[41] Later in this book you will hear a story that happened to me at a gathering like this, land even after 10 years of self-preparation and a variety of personal experiences, it still floored me.

CHANGING TACTICS

As it became apparent that the deck was too heavily stacked against us and that the Disclosure Project was not going to be able to break into the mainstream news no matter how good or compelling our evidence, the decision was made to concentrate on the Zero-Point Energy aspects of the UFO technology. We knew that if we were able to develop a ZPE energy system to a commercially viable level, we could release it to the public in such a way that the Genie could not be put back in the bottle. In the process we could change the entire fossil fuel and pollution paradigm, and dramatically shift the economies of the world away from the terrible drag of buying energy by the unit (Gallon, Kilowatt Hour, or BTU). The other advantage of this approach is that once we break into the mainstream media with the energy technology, they will start to ask where this technology came from. Then we will have an opening, a medium, and an audience, as well as the credibility to give the rest of the answer.

In connection with the energy aspects of the UFO/ET issue, I wrote this poem, to be read in the style of Dr. Seuss.

POWER FOR THE PEOPLE

Burning fossil fuels is quite bad,
It makes Mother Earth feel very sad.
Zero point energy is the elegant solution,
To most of mankind's awful pollution.

Clean distributed energy can help repair,
Much of humankind's current despair.
It can eliminate many of the reasons for,
This stupid thing that we call... WAR!

We can then come out of our shell,
And many things will start to get well.
Streams will run clean, the air will clear,
Humanity will then have much less to fear.

A vision of great hope and elation,
Will benefit each and every nation.
Peoples will learn how to get along,
And mankind will lift its voice in glorious song.

Peace and prosperity, better health for all,
Clean free energy can prevent civilizations disastrous fall.
A much brighter future our grandkids will see,
All because we had the courage to make energy... FREE!

PS. Somewhere in the universe a wise poet,
Helped with this verse, I know it.
That's the way it works, don't it,
Comes flooding in at an inspired moment.

© 2003 Don Daniels

About this time I was also interviewed by Hilly Rose for *Atlantis Rising Radio* (and the interview played on **Sirius** Radio, *hmm*, coincidence, I think not), talking primarily about the Geopolitical implications of the New Energy technology. That was my first nationwide interview (actually worldwide on the net), and once again I was stretching my comfort zone as I kind of got pushed into public speaking. I have been very careful to avoid mentioning, in most cases, that I am an airline pilot, and never allow anyone to state the name of the airline I work for. While the airline can't do much to me concerning what I do in my private life (as long as it is legal and moral), they can fire me if I associate the company name and my interest in subjects UFO.

As I got more into the Geopolitical implications of the whole UFO/ET/Energy paradigm, I found myself talking to a variety of people I would not have had the courage to even approach before. I talked to Dr. Maury Albertson, one of the founders of the Peace Corps and head of Village Earth and Hydrogen Now. Dr. Albertson also co-founded the International Association for New Science with Dr. Brian O'Leary and Dr. Bob Siblerud, among other projects. We met for lunch and had some very interesting exchanges. I have gleaned ideas from leaders of relief agencies in the Third World, and made policy suggestions to our groups based on that input. I have talked to the professor who wrote the famous "UFO" chapters in the Air Force training manual, and have photos of his personal copy of the book; one of only three or four copies left that did not have those chapters ripped out by the Air Force when it became publically known that they existed[42].

I saw an article in the English Pravda website about new energy technologies, so I asked the CSETI e-mail group if anyone knew someone in Russia that could verify the article and translation as valid, and wound up being a continuing pen pal with a Russian Peace Poet. I saw another article about a Russian scientist working in the new energy field, and simply wrote him a letter and got him in touch with our group leaders. I am no longer intimidated by position or national boundaries, as this is a worldwide problem we are trying to solve. My poet friend forwarded my letter written to the Bulletin of Atomic Scientists to Vladimir Putin. He was probably more receptive than our

---

[42]   See my website for photos of those pages from the Air Force Training Manual.

big oil administration of the time. As I grew internationally and geopolitically, I was inspired to write (or write down) this poem:

EVOLUTION

What is an average person to do,
when your government no longer represents you
You can deny it, or you can hide,
or you can fight, but you have to decide.

I am a citizen of the United States,
a party to all the great debates.
But it no longer makes me proud,
I feel compelled to speak my mind out loud.

My government does things in my name,
that make me drop my head in shame.
We didn't free Iraq for its masses,
but instead for the people that make auto gasses.

We humans are all much more the same
The major difference is in our name.
We all want the same outcome,
Peace, food, and hope for everyone.

I've considered myself a citizen of the World
Without national flag unfurled.
I feel more akin to the Afghan herder,
than to our leaders when they commit murder.

But then I met some people from afar
And discovered it matters not your home star.
So as I now conclude this short verse
I consider myself a citizen of the Universe.

© 2004 Don Daniels

In June of 2006 I was invited to attend a weekend retreat with Yug Purush Swami Parmanand Ji being held in nearby Bailey, Colorado. On one of the breaks I was visiting with Bob Keeton, the person who was recording the event, and found that he did a radio show on Sirius Satellite radio and Lime networks. I asked if he had ever interviewed Dr. Steven Greer, who just had a new book out at the time. He had previously interviewed Dr. Greer, but made a note of the new book. During the day we visited a bit more and I shared some of my UFO/ET experiences with him.

Sunday morning as we were taking a tea break at around 10 AM, Bob asked me if he could talk with me for a minute. I said "sure," so he dragged me out on the deck where his recording equipment was set up, stuck a mike in my face and started asking me questions. My thought was **"OH, you mean on the radio!"** Talk about an ambush interview, but it was one of the best I have ever given. I have to credit Bob Keeton for his insight and skillful interview techniques which helped me present a number of important points in a very fluid manner. You can still order a CD copy of that interview from www.livingsuccessfully.com and simply put my name in the search window.

Until 2006[43] I had continued to go out in the field at least once a year with the CSETI group to commune with our neighbors. I called it my "Reality Break" and it was my escape TO reality as opposed to the artificial "reality" we are fed by the mainstream media. To supplement the CSETI outings and work towards further contact on our own, I have organized a small Extraterrestrial Contact working group in the Denver area for the purpose of having local outings. In addition, I have worked on other projects such as developing a Pilot Survey with Dr. Richard Haines of NARCAP and formerly a psychologist with NASA. While I could not get approval to distribute this survey at my airline, a friend managed to get approval at another airline that returned not only very good data, but also an absolutely astounding return rate for a survey.

http://www.narcap.org/reports/005/narcap.survey.pdf

---

[43] While I learned a lot from CSETI between 1999 and 2006, I was starting to have differences of opinion on some issues, and decided it was time for me to branch out on my own. I organized a workshop with another contactee in which we had over 30 people attend, and again learned a lot. However, something told me it was time to stop riding other people's coattails and instead just make it happen on my own. So I dug in and started really working on myself and working with my small local research working group. It was after a few years of this that my biggest successes came.

I've been quoted in the British *UFO Magazine* from the Disclosure Conference, and asked to speak to various groups over the years following the Disclosure Project. There is no turning back at this point, I am out there in the world and there is no way to go except forward, but that is the only way I want to go anyway. I think the CSETI philosophy of "One Universe, One People" applies at all levels, from getting along with your neighbors to getting along with other nations to getting along with other species, both terrestrial and extraterrestrial.

When we all realize, as I have learned through experience and from talking to other witnesses, that at the most fundamental level we are all the same, we can learn to think of our visitors much as we would think of our Hispanic or Asian or Black neighbor or guest. They are awake and aware and conscious in the same way we are. They have similar hopes and dreams. Beyond sufficient food and shelter, they want a better future for their offspring and for all of creation. While they may be insectoid, reptilian, birdlike, mammalian, or possibly a form we have not yet imagined, and while they may have vastly different cultural and educational backgrounds, they are PEOPLE just like you and me. I have had telepathic contact with a number of species, and while most people would currently recoil at the sight of say a 6-foot tall Praying Mantis, I have found them to be very kind and gentle, at least in remote view conscious contact. In fact, they would probably sacrifice themselves rather than take a chance of injuring one of us. When humans evolve to this level of compassion and caring, we will automatically move beyond this paradigm of War we have been stuck in for millennia. Once we learn to get along with ourselves and stop shooting at our visitors, perhaps we will be invited to "Join the Cosmic Neighborhood!" I, for one, am way past ready for that!

CHAPTER EXERCISE: MEETING THE UNEXPECTED

Practice your basic "Oneness" meditation, but this time visualize how you would react if you met a Six Foot tall Praying Mantis. We have been programmed by the movies to fear the scary insectoid or reptilian ETs. The puppet masters of this world want to control the paradigm by making us fear contact, and fear prevents unconditional love and shuts down high-level contact immediately. Fear of anyone different from us has been used to pit one group of people against another for millennia. If you are putting out vibrations of Unconditional Love and Oneness, then that is what you will attract, and lower vibrational beings simply can't enter your space. Consider that on other worlds it is possible that other types of animals were the ones to evolve to higher consciousness, and this could be insects, reptiles, birds, sea mammals, or virtually any branch of animal biology. So put out Unconditional Love and Oneness to ANY being that resonates at those higher frequencies, and practice getting used to the possibility of finding yourself face to face with a very odd creature.

If this is too big a leap, start by simply noticing your "First Impression" of others as you walk down the street or meet people in different places. If you were a product of the '60s and '70s like I was, then we were programmed with a fair amount of racism just by watching the evening news about the race riots that were going on. We are all heavily influenced by events and attitudes that prevailed in our early years, especially our teen years. Often the times change, but we still have this old behavioral and attitude conditioning deep within us at a subconscious level. It may be one aspect of our personality that we sincerely wish to modify, so you can start by simply analyzing your first impressions of people. If you discover some prejudice creeping through, self-correct and tell yourself that your first impression was not fair. Remind yourself that you strive to treat EVERYONE as equal and give EVERYONE the benefit of the doubt, at least until they prove you wrong. In this way, we can start to change our attitudes so that we can also meet an Extraterrestrial with an open mind and without prejudice, no matter how they appear.

CLOSE ENCOUNTERS OF THE CRUSTACEAN KIND!

July 4th, 2005

Out in the field on one of my later CSETI trainings, we were having a very interesting night. We had very specific repeated light flashes from four different directions in deep space, subtle lights, non-physical forms within the group, and much more. Toward the end of the evening we had been seeing deep space flashes (I call them Flash Bulb effect, similar to an older photo flashbulb, more yellow and slightly longer duration than the modern strobe lights), and then settled down into meditation to try to remote view whoever was around and seemed to be trying to interact with us. I have had some success with this in the past, but had been frustrated for the last couple of years.

I settled into my chair and dove deeply into the sea of pure consciousness. I was tired from a whole week of staying out until 2 AM, and did not have the energy for the full CSETI protocol, so I simply mentally invited our friends to "come on down and play," or, as an after-thought, added, "or beam me up." **INSTANTLY**, with no sense of time, distance, or travel, I found myself (at least in consciousness or astral body) in some kind of control room on what appeared to be a craft, surrounded by ten or fifteen small crustacean humanoid creatures about 3 feet tall. While the instant transition was a bit of a surprise, I was in a state of consciousness where I felt no fear of any kind, and didn't even experience an adrenaline rush, but instead remained at all times perfectly comfortable with the situation.

My first thought was that I was towering over these beings and I wondered if this might be intimidating to them, so I got down on my knees and then sat down on the floor so I was at their level, just like you do with young kids. This also conveyed that I intend no threat or harm to them, and hopefully put them more at ease with me. Their faces reminded me of Crawdads, but with a skinny neck, skinny bodies, and long skinny arms and legs. They were making a gentle clicking speech (similar to the unique throat clicking language of the Bushmen of the Kalahari, interesting?), and there was a soft clacking noise from their pincher type hands.

They were gathering around me like a bunch of curious children, and several very gently approached and touched me very carefully and lovingly with their crab-like hands, just like a blind person feeling your face to get an idea what you look like. Looking back, it is amazing that I felt no fear or apprehension of any kind, but the feeling was very comfortable and loving. The Compassion, Concern and Curiosity were very palpable, and I just **knew** that I was totally safe. I got the impression they were curious about what this human was doing and why he was putting himself out in this situation on purpose. As they were doing this, I said (mentally in thought form) that I didn't know the proper greeting in their culture, and I got back a thought or impression that my mind translated as "You are doing fine!" Then someone back in the CSETI group in the Baca exclaimed abruptly about a nice meteor they saw, and I snapped back into my body very abruptly and even a bit painfully. In an instant I was back in the circle of people under the stars. I had this fleeting "Nooo, I want to go back" feeling of disappointment that the link was severed so quickly, but what is time in those realms anyway? I was just disappointed that the encounter was over so quickly.

Looking back, there are several amazing things that occurred. I had been training myself for years in the CSETI program to act and react appropriately as an "Ambassador to the Universe," and part of that includes being able to approach high strangeness events without fear. Another aspect is to treat others with respect and understand the fundamental oneness of all beings, regardless of what they look like. In consciousness we are all connected to the same source, the same Universal Consciousness, and from that basis we can start to build a mutually respectful relationship. This is the origin of the CSETI slogan **"One Universe, One People."**

Well, I was really put to the test in those few moments. Once I had the flash of inspiration to basically allow them to beam me up, and effectively gave them permission, I was INSTANTLY there with them. In retrospect, it makes great sense to meet them halfway, on their home turf, rather than in the hostile military environment of Earth. This was much easier and safer for them, and probably helped facilitate the contact.

Examine in your own mind how you would react if you found yourself suddenly surrounded by 3 foot tall crustaceans with pincher hands. I think that was an indication of how well I had prepared myself. My first thought was that I must appear intimidating to them. I was considerate of their feelings first. I came down to their level physically, putting myself in a trusting and vulnerable position to again meet them halfway.

I accepted their loving gentle touch, and inquired about the proper greeting in their culture. By greeting them in this manner, with humility and respect, I had opened the door to a mutually respectful relationship. If this was the final exam for "Ambassadors to the Universe" training on Earth, I think I passed, and I feel I am ready to move on to further assignments.

Let's get on with transforming this planet and joining the galactic and universal community that we are a part of. It is our destiny that we become enlightened peoples, connected in God Consciousness to the oneness of all creation. This is currently denied us by those who crave power and control over others. Those who want us to look outward to them for answers will simply become irrelevant in the new paradigm. Almost everyone will learn how to look inward for their own answers and act accordingly. As the masses of humanity grow into full consciousness, they will become self-governing, and at the same time ungovernable. This is one thing that governments fear, for as we grow as individuals, governments at the same time become increasingly irrelevant.

Our future is as highly conscious, empowered beings that will eventually go out into the cosmos to help other civilizations grow and evolve. It is a great and important task for which we will be well suited. We need to look upon ourselves as **Humans Becoming**, and then become all that we can be and truly already are!

May we Create Peace Profound.

CHAPTER EXERCISE: HIGH STRANGENESS

Work some more on your Oneness meditation, and then practice in meditation getting used to meeting creatures that are very different from us. You might review some event in your life where you overcame a fear. Perhaps you had, for example, a fear of dogs, and yet with practice you were able to overcome this fear and now are comfortable around and relate well with dogs.

Once you have that concept in mind, consider meeting other species of Extraterrestrials either in Remote Viewing, Out of Body, or eventually in physical form. Practice remaining calm with the encounter, and remind yourself that they are awake and aware and conscious in much the same way as you. Consider that they are connected to the same source as you, and in that way they are fundamentally connected to you.

Understand that they probably have the same basic wants and needs as you, most likely a desire for peace, possibly food, and the hope for a better future for their kids. See them as not fundamentally much different than the family who just moved into your neighborhood from some far flung corner of the globe. You probably have a lot more in common than you realize.

Now see, that wasn't so scary after all, was it?

PHYSIOLOGICAL EFFECTS OF CONTACT AND HOW TO HANDLE THEM

OK, while I have not had any serious physiological side effects from my encounters, others I know have. So I will share what I have learned about this from others.

First of all, I think that adequate preparation is the first line of defense. But can I say that if I were to experience a landing event and have a face-to-face physical encounter with a rather non-human species that I would be totally calm and collected? Probably not! There would be a lot of excitement, possibly some fear from prior programming that would creep through in this kind of highly charged situation, and perhaps a bit of the deeply ingrained "Fight or Flight" impulse. However, I would be better prepared than most, and more able to regain my composure. Also, we understand that they are sensitive to our feelings, and all indications are that first we will be introduced to others who look very much like us, and after we get used to that idea we will start to meet species who are more different.

If you are fortunate enough to have an encounter of your own in the near future, it may be helpful to have some coping skills ready. If you have already had an encounter, then just reviewing your response to those prior events is likely to be helpful. How did you do? Did you freak out or were you reasonably controlled? Would you handle things differently now that you have the advantage of hindsight and introspection? Are you ready for another encounter, or do you need to do more work to prepare yourself?

Many people recommend breathing through an encounter, since focusing on your breathing gives you a point of reference you can anchor to. If you have practiced my basic Oneness breathing meditation enough that it is natural and easy, you will have just such a skill. Then if things get weird or disorienting, you can focus on a few breaths and rapidly and easily drop into that silence between the breaths, moving right into

Oneness and Unconditional Love. From this point of reference you can hopefully approach your encounter in a much more positive frame of reference, rather than blocking it right from the start with a fear response.

Perhaps part of this goes back to my early high school Ski Racing training. When things start to happen very fast for you, like in a downhill ski race, it is easy to FORGET to breathe. Lack of adequate oxygen causes hypoxia, and a common side effect of hypoxia is a feeling of anxiety. HMMM! Perhaps in an intense encounter you forget to breathe, get hypoxic, and the anxiety is from a lack of oxygen as much as from the encounter itself. BREATHE!

It is also sometimes helpful to change your frame of reference a bit. For Slalom or Giant Slalom races we generally thought of ourselves as moving down the hill toward the gates, but in Downhill racing it helped to think of the terrain coming up to you. I am approaching this gate in slalom, but this corner is coming up towards me in a downhill course. Subtle, but perhaps you can apply something similar to see yourself as more of a detached observer in an encounter if it is getting too intense for your comfort.

Once that physiological "Fight or Flight" response kicks in, it is difficult to back out of that mode and salvage the situation. It may be possible if you recognize what is happening, ask for a little time and space to get collected, and breathe. It might help both you and your visitors if you state your intention to try to continue the encounter, and work to calm yourself so that you can continue. They seem very respectful of our feelings, and generally the least psychologically prepared person in the group is the limiting factor. As soon as someone starts to get uncomfortable, that seems to set the extent of the encounter. If you have made all the effort to prepare yourself to the extent that they noticed and came all this way to meet with you, then I would expect that they would stand off at a respectful distance and give you time to compose yourself if you asked and are trying to make it work. They understand more than you know.

WHO'S WHO?

Many people talk about the Greys, Reptilians and others, and popular culture often portrays them as evil. Movies often portray Insectoid ETs as ruthless invaders. Some people insist they have been abducted. Where is the truth in all of this?

As I have stated, you attract what you put out, and thus, fortunately I have had no interaction with any entities that were any less than the highest ethics[44]. As a result, this chapter is based on information from outside sources, intuitions, and information received telepathically or channeled by others.

There have been Extraterrestrial contacts already, both with individuals and reportedly with governments, and some of these meetings have reportedly gone better than others.

There is a story that two different groups of Extraterrestrials approached our US government back in the '40s or '50s; one with very high ethics who offered technologies to help us clean up our polluted environment, and the other that offered technologies that could be used to gain military advantage in exchange for reportedly less altruistic goals.

Col. Phillip Corso[45] reportedly had an encounter with extraterrestrials out in the desert, and was offered a chance to work with them toward various goals for the benefit of Earth. Near the end of the conversation he asked, "What's in it for me?" The response was "A better world, if you can take it." I'm sure in his later years Col. Corso probably regretted not only failing to take the offer, but even asking the question.

---

[44] If you prefer, you can start your contact attempts with a statement or intention that you wish to only work with entities of the highest ethics, those that are working in the Light and for the best interest of humanity and the Earth.

[45] *The Day After Roswell*—Col. Phillip Corso

Who are the Greys? There are many theories running around, but the one that makes the most sense to me is what Bashar[46] says in channeled communications through Darryl Anka. Bashar says that the Greys are not technically Extra-terrestrial, but are from a Parallel Earth that destroyed its environment. In order to survive, they had to mutate, and in the mutation process they lost the ability to procreate. Bashar says they are coming to our Earth to get genetic material for creating a hybrid species, and that our family bloodlines are nearly identical to those in their parallel world. This is supposedly why "abductions" tend to run in families. There is generally a soul-level (pre-birth) contract to participate with them in helping them rebuild their species, though often we don't remember that agreement when the experiences occur.

Since they often attempt to work during our sleep, it is often hard to distinguish these experiences from a dream, if there is any memory at all. It would perhaps be a bit more ethical if they explicitly asked permission for our cooperation, but they would probably get a lot of refusals from freaked-out people, especially with all the scary abduction stories and movies that are going around. My opinion is that the emotionally charged term "Abduction" is used in many cases of much more mutually consensual or respectful encounters, simply because the reporters have been indoctrinated by the media to only know that term to describe their experience. Very little is reported of any less scary or even peaceful and loving encounters, even though I believe many of these actually occur with equal or greater frequency.

The Greys are said to lack emotion, and are trying to get that attribute back in the hybrids. They are in many ways similar to us, scientific and intelligent. Some say they are without spirituality or even soulless. In this respect they are said to be less ethical than the true Extra-terrestrials of the Alliance that are said to be working with us to help with our evolution and ascension to higher dimensions.

In my mind it is also possible that they, like us, allowed their technology to outpace their spirituality, and in that way almost destroyed themselves. Perhaps they are trying to help us avoid the same mistakes, and to encourage us to keep our technology under control and used only for good purposes. Maybe they are trying to share lessons learned.

There are also reports of cloned Bio-mechanical entities being created by covert human projects. These are reportedly being used in hoaxed abduction scenarios of targeted people, and this perhaps

---

[46]   www.bashar.org

accounts for the cold, soulless feeling encountered by some "Abductees." These types are sometimes reported to glide over the ground rather than walk.

Another subject of discussion is the supposed Reptilian Shape Shifters that some claim have infiltrated our governments and secretly ruled our world for millennia. This group is supposed to be greedy, ruthless and manipulative. They supposedly manipulate us with fear, and some say they even feed off of this fear to give themselves energy. Do they exist and are these stories true? I really don't know, having never had dealings with them that I know of. I do know that the peoples of our planet have been manipulated by fear for ages, and I for one am way past ready to move beyond that to a new paradigm of education, cooperation, and mutually beneficial solutions to our problems.

As far as emotion among the extraterrestrials is concerned, remember that my encounters for the first several years were entirely on the level of emotional communication. At least the peoples I have encountered seemed to have souls and highly developed emotions, so in my experience you could not say they were lacking souls or emotions. Anyone who makes a blanket statement to that effect is, in my opinion, either egocentric, anthropocentric, or has a limited experience base upon which to draw that conclusion. Remember that throughout recorded history humans were always taught to believe that we were special or superior in various ways to anything or anyone different from ourselves or our group, clan, nation or species. That will take some time to change.

Insectoids! What could be scarier for Hollywood or Psy-Ops disinformation specialists than super large, scary-looking bugs attacking us?

Speaking of Psy-Ops, let us remember that good disinformation is 80-90% true. If you have a phenomenon that you can't contain, like Crop Circles for instance, you try to discredit them by hoaxing or encouraging a few people to hoax some, and then you prove those as hoaxes, hoping that the vast majority of the people will throw the baby out with the bath water. In this way you can create doubt about the real events that you can't prevent.

The same principle is used to discredit UFO/ET reports. For instance, there was a widely circulated report about the UFO over Chicago's O'Hare airport a few years ago. There were many witnesses and even some purported photographs. One reporter was supposedly a ramp worker for one of the major airlines. The guy sounded credible, knew the lingo of the airport ramp workers, and he got a lot of air time. But when I listened to his story, I caught a couple of ringers in his report that got my attention. For instance, he said he was headed to the F concourse to load a 727. Well, that particular airline used the F gates only for regional jet express carriers, and had parked all of its Boeing 727's a number of years earlier after 9/11 and no longer even flew that type airplane. My radar went up immediately that this was a disinformation attempt and that the factual errors would later be pointed out. In this way people would be led to believe it was all a hoax or didn't really happen, even though there was much evidence that the event was real.

Back to different species of Extraterrestrials, my understanding is that any major animal group can become dominant on a given planet and evolve to higher consciousness. An upright posture seems to prevail, something about a vertical energy flow through the chakras contributing to higher consciousness, but the Cetaceans have also developed a very high level of consciousness while oriented mostly horizontal. It is helpful to remember at this point that no matter what the body type, all higher consciousness beings are sparked by the same seed of consciousness, by the same creator, and in this way we are all connected.

I would prefer to give them the benefit of the doubt no matter what they looked like, and attempt to create a peaceful relationship with them. Think of it this way: If they are peaceful and we are hostile, we muck it up. If they are hostile or neutral and we are peaceful, we stand a chance of changing their mind about us. In the worst case, if we meet hostility with hostility, we will most likely lose since they already have the technology to travel interstellar and thus potentially have weapons far superior to ours. The only logical approach I see is to try peaceful interaction first, as it holds the only viable outcomes. Either we get a win-win if they are also peaceful, or we stand a chance of converting it to a good solution if they are neutral or slightly hostile. I'm not saying give them our planet or anything like that. I'm just saying that approaching first contact from a position of fear and conflict has very few, if any, positive outcomes.

CHAPTER EXERCISE: PSYCHOLOGICAL CHARACTER STUDY

Rent, borrow, or buy the movie *The Day the Earth Stood Still*. Not the remake, that was awful, but the original with Michael Rennie, made in 1951, http://www.imdb.com/title/tt0043456/. Get the collector's edition if you can, the one that has the director's comments.

Now, watch it again for the first time!

Watch it with the understanding that it was an educational film and a psychological character study put out by the good guys at the State Department in an effort to get people thinking about how they should react to such an occurrence as an extraterrestrial visitor to Earth. Notice the reaction of the military, the scientist, the doctors, the government officials, and the civilians. How does each group react to the news of an extraterrestrial visitor? Who acted out of fear, and who out of compassion and an attempt to understand? Pay attention to the message that we cannot keep on going the way we have been behaving if we wish to survive as a civilization.

And then contrast this with some of the scary invading alien movies you may have seen, think about the messages they may have been trying to portray and what the ulterior motive to those messages may have been. Might the message be "Be afraid so we can control you"? Fear shuts down your ability to enter the higher levels of consciousness that are necessary in order to have contact, or even to evolve spiritually. People wanting to control us know that if we can be made afraid, we can be prevented from having our own contact and learning the larger truths that would topple their carefully constructed power structures. There is a lot at stake for some in keeping us afraid and ignorant. But you don't have to give them your power; you can go forward without fear and find your own truth.

Courage fortifying note: If you understand that our consciousness goes on forever, and that we don't truly die but simply change dimensions or levels of consciousness, then it makes it easier to go boldly (yet with appropriate caution) into the unknown. Explore with courage and with the knowledge that if you put out unconditional love and gratitude, then that is what you will find in return. In this way you can feel safe and protected in your own search for truth.

THE CONCEPT OF DIMENSIONS

Recently I took a workshop on Out-of-Body travel put on by William Buhlman[47], and while talking with him during one of the breaks, I shared my Crustacean Contact experience with him. He pointed out that the experience was tactile, that I could feel them touching me, and that therefore meant the experience was a spontaneous "Out-of-Body" encounter rather than just a remote view. If I could feel them touching me, my astral body had to have been there. Interesting!

Take a few minutes to reflect on your life, and consider the possibility that you may have experienced an out-of-body experience, perhaps even one you did not recognize as such. Common "symptoms" include a loud buzzing or rushing noise, a body vibration (often strong), or a sense that the walls or other physical objects around you are dissolving or becoming fluid. You may find that you can lift up or roll out of your body, though looking back at yourself or just thinking about your physical body often results in an immediate snap-back into the body. In my case none of these more dramatic effects occurred, I was just instantly "there!" Sometimes there is a rush of movement or an effect like traveling through a tunnel. If you try to move around, you may find that you can move merely by thinking. Sometimes you see your house as very similar to what you know, only with minor differences. Sometimes you feel you are in a dream, but you can "feel" things around you or people touching you. If you have experienced any of these things, it is possible you have had an out-of-body experience.

To expand just a little bit on dimensions, William Buhlman relates the different dimensions or realms to different levels of consciousness or different vibrations. He says that what we call the physical 3rd dimension, where we spend most of our time, is actually the outermost densest crust of the Multiverse. As we move inward in consciousness and higher in

---

[47] **http://www.out-of-body.com** Adventures Beyond the Body

vibration, we move through different realms. They range in a relative continuum from our dense physical consensus reality to lighter density, though still physical appearing realms, to increasingly thought responsive realms, to realms of pure energy and consciousness without form.

The near astral realm, just barely shifted up from our Physical realm, is where people reportedly go initially when they pass through transition. It appears very similar to what we are used to when fully in the physical conscious state. Things appear solid and physical, though the careful observer might notice slight differences. Then the light comes for these souls, guides and relatives are present, and most people go into the light to higher (frequency) realms where they rest, do a life review to understand lessons learned and lessons left, and plan for their next incarnation if desired.

Many people get stuck in the near astral because it is familiar and they even see a near duplicate of the things they are familiar with, their house and such. They become attached to the familiar and are afraid to go into the light and into the unknown. Sometimes they hang around and even feed off the energies of those they left behind. Some people who are talented OBE explorers and healers will engage in a practice called "Soul Rescue," where they travel to the near astral, find these trapped souls, and help them move up to a point of consciousness where they can see their guides and move into the light and the higher realms where they belong. (*Don't try this at home until you are pretty competent and confident in your own abilities to handle unknown situations and are experienced enough to navigate proficiently when out of body*).

How does this apply to Extraterrestrial Contact? Many, if not most of those entities visiting us are living, or at least able to operate, in the higher frequency and more energetic realms. This is where it is much easier to travel, and where they are safer from our violence. For several reasons those who come into our realm may find it hard to become fully physical to interact with us. It is very much like moving down into darkness and lower emotions, and is not only distasteful, but physically difficult for them. Imagine yourself as a light worker and healer having to descend into the pits of violence and hatred of a ruthless civil war. You would find that distasteful. And so, for them to come from what might be termed the 5th dimension to our level of fear, hatred, distrust, and violence is equally distasteful, and yet some of them are so dedicated to humanity and our growth and evolution that they make that commitment anyway. These individuals who live and work among us are truly brave and dedicated souls leading a very lonely life. More on this will be covered in the next chapter.

But first, since it is difficult for our visitors to come all the way down to our level, we have to learn how to lift ourselves up in order to meet them halfway. So how do we do this? I have been giving you a series of practice exercises with each chapter so far, and if you have been working on them, that should have you already making good progress. At this point we will focus on tying it all together and giving you an overview, or big picture, of what has worked to enable high level contact experiences for myself and others.

There are many paths up the mountain, so I will talk about what has worked for me personally and offer some other suggestions. In general, it is a path to spiritual enlightenment which involves serious introspection and self-analysis. It is a matter of being aware of your own thoughts, and knowing that those thoughts have effects. Thus you will understand that it is wise to become disciplined in your thinking. If you are bouncing all over the place with a wide range of random thoughts, including fear and thoughts of violence, then telepathing with you would be like you trying to have a conversation with a delusional psychopath, not very comfortable or productive for them. Also, as you move into higher vibrational realms, the environment becomes increasingly *Thought Responsive*, so your random thoughts might manifest very rapidly. For these reasons mental discipline could not only make you more desirable for them to interact with, but it might also prevent some unpleasant surprises of your own creation.

I suggest you take some kind of mystical path, for me it was the Rosicrucian studies. Learn meditation, introspection, morals and ethics. With the introspection often comes what is termed "The Dark Night of the Soul," for when you start to look at yourself honestly you inevitably find things you do not like. This period of self-discovery can be quite disturbing, and it is easy to become depressed at this point. Here it is very helpful to have a support mechanism to back you up and encourage you as you move forward through the alchemical cleansing of the soul. You will come out the far side a better person, having discarded the dross of lower thinking. This "Dark Night" or period of feeling overwhelmed or depressed is a very common occurrence on the path to enlightenment. Know that if you can stick with it, things will get much better soon.

Now that you are aware of your own thoughts and have gained some level of discipline over them, you can start working on considering all people as equals. They are awake and aware and conscious in the same way as we are, sparked by the same seed of consciousness as us and by the same Source or Creator. When we realize that we are all fundamentally connected in that same way, it becomes fundamentally wrong to take advantage of or harm another person. With this understanding we can move into a state of fundamental Oneness. Understanding that we are all creations of the same source, we can see all with Unconditional Love. If you have trouble with the concept of unconditional love, just consider a puppy dog and how it loves you unconditionally, or your love of your kids, and how even if they make mistakes, you still love them and want them to succeed. Now apply this level of Unconditional Love to any Extra-terrestrial visitors you might meet, knowing that most likely they will have come a very long way to work with us toward the advancement of humanity and the preservation of our planet. For this we owe them our gratitude.

Now that you are able to view our visitors with unconditional love and an understanding of our fundamental oneness, you are automatically in a state of higher "vibration" emanating these higher emotions, and thus you are also free of any thoughts of fear, hatred or violence.

Remember, in some theories we were colonists from their worlds, so they could literally be our biological cousins! It is in this state where we can meet our visitors halfway. They will notice your efforts and respond to the extent they can and at the level that you are ready for. This is how it began for me, and while it seemed to be a painfully slow process over a period of 10 years, it has moved me continuously through different experiences and has paid huge dividends, especially in recent years. I've been told that our efforts are noticed at the highest levels, and are greatly appreciated. Even though it doesn't pay the rent, working toward improved relations between us and our visitors is very rewarding in other ways. If you work sincerely to prepare yourself and take these lessons to heart, you will be ready to fill one of many important diplomatic or educational roles here on Earth when open contact starts to occur.

CHAPTER EXERCISE: MOVING INWARD TO REACH OUT!

Contemplate the concept of Moving Inward to reach out. William Buhlman says that in order to reach the higher dimensions, the higher frequency realms that become increasingly more thought responsive, we have to go deeper INWARD! Inscribed on the Temple of Apollo at Delphi is inscribed the injunction, "Know Thyself, and though shalt Know the Gods." The latter part is often left off, but perhaps the deeper meaning can be deduced from the following quote:

"The best known Delphic injunction was carved into the lintel at the Temple of Apollo: GNOTHI SEAUTON, Know Thyself. These words may have originated in Apollo's response to a question Chilon of Sparta asked: 'What is best for man?' The reply, 'Know thyself,' is similar to the one believed to have been given to the Lydian king, Croesus, when he was told that he must know himself if he would live most happily. Croesus, a man of action and not philosophical, took this to mean that he should know his own strength, know what he wanted, and should rely on his own judgment. Others have found deeper meaning in these words, taking the 'self' to mean the higher self, the true Self; to imply that as man is the microcosm of the macrocosm, he who knows himself knows all."[48]

One can apply the old injunction "As Above, So Below" and infer that by going deep within oneself, one can tap into a connection with deeper knowledge, the Akashic Records. It is a level of consciousness where all that was, is, or will be is recorded and accessible to those who are able, and thus they can "Know Themselves." In some interpretations, the Akashic Records actually consist of a direct connection to the "Mind of God!" Taken from the perspective of a Holographic Universe, WE are a holographic snippet of the universe, containing *all that is* within us. Viewed from the other perspective, every part of the Universe thus also contains a snippet of us. If we can connect with that aspect of ourselves, we can gain access to much more than ourselves.

---

[48] http://www.theosophy-nw.org/theosnw/world/med/me-elo.htm

Let's try a meditation on this concept. I like the basic breathing meditation, going into the silence between the breaths in order to move within. Focus on Unconditional Love and Oneness to raise your personal vibrations to a higher level, and then contemplate the concept of the Akashic Records. Pose the question, "What are the Akashic Records?" and then become receptive to inspiration and impressions. Just be in oneness with the wisdom of the universe for a period of time, and then slowly return to normal consciousness. Make note of your impressions, but also be alert for impressions that may filter in over the next several days.

If you are successful, you may develop an ability to tap into the wisdom of the universe, and find answers that are beyond yourself. I suggest repeating this exercise several times, adding in questions that you are seeking inspiration on.

AN UNEXPECTED SURPRISE

For some time, I was wondering where this would all lead, and wanting more definitive contact. Even though I thought I was ready, each gradual new phase of contact still brought about a paradigm shift in my being, and I just had to trust that everything was happening at the proper pace. While I thought I was ready to have, for instance, a craft land and physical beings walk out and greet us, it seems the cosmic and higher dimensions had other plans.

It was being pointed out to me in various ways that I was somewhat of a connector. People kept running into me, and I would connect them with whom or what they were looking for. One example: I was strangely drawn, almost compelled, to attend a mini-class in Soul Regression Therapy at the local metaphysical "College in Morrison." Not really sure why I was there other than the topic sounded intriguing, I listened to the presentation, considered setting up a session, and visited with the presenter and some of the attendees.

During the question and answer session, a woman behind me asked if anyone knew of Mark Kimble and how to get in touch with him, as he was doing some workshops she was interested in. I asked if she meant Mark Kimmel. The details of what she was looking for matched, so I gave her the contact information. Lo and behold, sometime later we met at a gathering Mark was putting on. While I hardly remembered connecting her with Mark, she was convinced that she had been drawn to that same Soul Regression Therapy presentation for the purpose of meeting me and thus connecting with Mark Kimmel. This is just one of many connections I have made over the years, and one of many ways I have been told I have changed people's lives, propelling them on journeys of exploration and enlightenment or giving them the courage to speak their own truth.

Many times when sharing my experiences with others, it has triggered the release of experiences that for years they have had bottled up inside themselves for fear of ridicule. If I share my story first, and am thus vulnerable, and do this in an environment in which they then feel safe to share their own experiences, the unloading can be incredibly healing for them. Often it is more like a Ram Dump as the experiences just pour out of them.

Perhaps this is part of my mission, to take the risk and push the envelope a bit so that others can heal. This has not been without repercussions, but it has been worth it in many ways. One fellow pilot fell rapidly into the pre-conditioned ridicule mode, but when I didn't falter, he started to tell me about an experience his wife had many years ago as a child overseas. Well, the more we talked, the more open he started to become, to the point where he had his wife meet us for dinner on a layover a couple days later. While he still ridiculed his wife's story (which must have been a bit hard on the relationship), he was now interested in my take on it, and wanted me to meet his wife.

At dinner, I started by sharing some of my experiences to let her know that I would not laugh at hers, but would take her seriously. You could see the barriers coming down, and finally she relayed a story about when she was quite young and living in Southeast Asia. Her father had had a flat tire along the highway. It was a terribly hot day, and while her father was changing the tire and she was watching, a platform only a few feet per side with a railing flew out from a nearby hill, stopped, and hovered nearby. From her experience it looked like a baby crib. Standing on the platform and holding onto the railing, there was a being who looked them over, and then the platform flew back to where it had come from. She felt it was checking to make sure they were OK. It hovered noiselessly, and she did not think her father saw it. Well, when I said that I had seen a wide variety of things and that this seemed entirely possible, you could see her shoulders rise as if a ton of weight had just been lifted. I was perhaps the first person in her life to consider the possibility of the event being real, as opposed to her suffering ridicule and questions of sanity. You could see that it was a significant healing experience for her. While hubby was still having trouble shaking off the Psy-Ops conditioned "giggle and ridicule" mode, he was starting to come around and consider the possibilities. There was progress there too, in smaller steps, but progress.

Toward this end, we have on occasion organized weekend gatherings, specifically for this purpose of bringing people together that have had UFO/ET encounters. We create a safe, private environment for them, and then share some of our insights on the topic. As people become more comfortable, they are encouraged to also share their stories with the group and thus dump the heavy burden they have been carrying, some-times for many years. A lot of healing and acceptance takes place, both in mutually supporting each other, and in accepting their own experiences. Most people feel that they are all alone in these experiences, and to have a support network of others with similar experiences is very helpful.

I had also met another person who seemed rather reserved, but as I talked about my experiences she opened up just a touch and intimated an experience in her youth, one that had been rather traumatic due to subsequent encounters with Project Blue Book military officers. She didn't want to open up more than that at the time, but I invited her out to a gathering that was occurring in a few months. She reluctantly accepted the invitation, arrangements were made, and despite almost chickening out, she did arrive. Others were at the gathering that I had "unconsciously" connected in ways similar to what I described previously. There was a diverse mix of people who were there for a wide range of reasons. Some were there to learn, share, release, and grow personally. Some were there seeking validation of events in their lives that they perhaps didn't quite believe themselves. Some were even adversarial about what we were sharing, perhaps because they didn't believe their own experiences either. Some of us were there primarily to facilitate the healing, already being comfortable in our own truths. Some did not fit with the group or had other commitments and did not return for the Sunday session, as is sometimes common, but as we were to learn, this was as it was intended.

Toward the end of the last day of our gathering, and while we were talking about how to prepare for the coming planetary shifts, I suggested to Tashina[49] that I really suspected there was a lot more to her story than she had shared with us so far, and asked if she would now feel comfortable sharing a bit more with the group. The intent was to allow her to get the burden off her shoulders in a supporting environment, as the remaining group had bonded quite nicely. Well, the next thing that happened just about blew me away. She took a very deep breath and started off by saying that **"Earth is a very difficult assignment!"** As this started to sink in, my jaw just slowly hit the floor. This person, whom I had thought was a human who had had a UFO/ET encounter, was just about the opposite. As she continued, she said she had been sent to Colorado by her "guides/supervisors" to meet someone who could help

---

[49]   She claimed to be from an unnamed 5th Dimensional world, and now says she is Arcturian. I originally gave her the pseudonym "Sarah 5" due to her similarity to the heroine in Mark Kimmel's *Trillion* trilogy[50]. She has since asked that I use her spiritual name Tashina in the book instead.

her move out into mainstream society, able to function and blend in so that she could accomplish her mission. It was apparent to her now that I was the person she had been sent to meet. Whoa! Major ego/burden/paradigm shift occurring all at once and the "Oh My Gods" were coming at a rate of one every few seconds. Boy, was I knocked off balance yet again! I had been working at putting the ego in perspective, but being told that not only were some ETs not omnipotent and all knowing, but also that I had been chosen by those in higher dimensions[50] to assist one of their own, who was living among us, was quite unexpected news. That caused all kinds of confusion and quite a swirl of emotions.

Wow! The implications were zinging around in my head, wanting to tell the world as I am very open with my truth, but also realizing that the world wasn't quite ready for this. More importantly, to protect her safety and her mission, it would be necessary to keep it a secret for a while. Keeping secrets is not in my nature, and this was to become very difficult for me. I had healed so many by sharing my truth and by advocating that they talk freely about their experiences in a safe environment. Suddenly I had one of the biggest truths around and couldn't even talk about it. For me, that IS very tough!

Hugs and tears flowed freely as we brought the gathering to a close and said our goodbyes[51]. We felt great appreciation for what this "person" had sacrificed personally (basically a lifetime) in order to try to help humanity evolve and grow up. While her mission and focus was nurturing the new generation of gifted human children and helping them to reach their full potential, specifics need to be kept secret for now to avoid identifying her, or others like her, to the puppet masters of our world. Imagine if the wrong people found her! At the very least they would want to detain and study her, and I don't even want to think about the worst they might do. Our puppet masters know it would be more difficult to keep us all subjugated and under their control as compliant little sheeple if we were aware of this larger reality. For now it is best to just keep quiet about the details and to assist these benevolent ET visitors whenever it is mutually beneficial and in whatever ways I am able. We did manage to find creative solutions to several of her problems, by the way.

---

[50] **www.CosmicParadigm.com** *Trillion, Decimal* and *One. Trillion* was so similar to my experiences that I helped Mark with ideas and editing on the remaining two books. They are a great "Faction" (Fact based Action Adventure Science Fiction) read, and real page turners.

[51] Yes, you can touch them, they don't break! In fact, Tashina gave great hugs of appreciation for our help and understanding.

I have long held that as humanity grows spiritually, we become both more self-governing, and at the same time more un-governable. The old paradigms and structures[52] lose their significance, and as the people reach an enlightened critical mass, they will start to demand changes in the basic governmental, economic and educational structures of our world[53]. I think this is what those in control of this world fear the most. Well, it seems this ET and I are both working to foster similar growth, so I guess that makes us a threat to the puppet masters of the current paradigm. Tough for them!

In order to communicate more securely with Tashina, we set up an encrypted online chat link. When we first tried it, I could hear her but she couldn't hear me. As soon as I figured out she was not hearing me, I jumped into the text window and started typing answers furiously to her questions. After about the third answer, she started laughing hysterically. I furiously typed, "What's so funny?" to which she replied verbally that "My telepathy was working a lot better than my typing." Oh well! I guess I am a better sender than receiver, but it also became totally apparent that there would be no secrets from her, and total honesty was the order of the relationship.

Tashina and our cat El bonded instantly and became best friends. A couple of weeks before we were planning to meet again, the vet found some marble size tumors in El's mammary glands, probably cancer from laying on top of the old CRT computer monitor where it was warm. I mentioned this to Tashina and told her we were leaving the cat at the vet for surgery when we left town to meet up. The day surgery was scheduled, I called the vet to check on how it went, and she was all perplexed. She confirmed that she had shown us the tumors, which she had. She said she didn't understand it, but could find no tumors at this time, and so she didn't operate. I looked at Tashina and asked if she had done something

---

[52] **http://www.cosmicparadigm.com/Books/Transformation/** Mark's latest book *Transformation* has a good description of the "Structures" we have allowed to control our lives, and some alternative ways from other civilizations. Easy to navigate by topic and in E-book download format, it is very reasonably priced. Also check out **http://cosmicparadigm.com/Athabantian/** for more current information as it comes in.

[53] Consider the Arab Spring, the populist revolts in Europe, the Wisconsin recall elections in the US, and now public demonstrations all over the world demanding truth and honesty in government and business. It is already happening all around the world and increasingly here in the US where movements like Occupy Wall Street and Move Your Money are gaining momentum. It is just not widely reported by the corporate controlled press, who get their advertising revenue from these same big banks and corporations.

for our kitty. She looked a little sheepish and nodded her head yes. Well, thank you! I told the vet that was fine and we would pick El up in a couple of days. Somehow Tashina had cured our cat of probable breast cancer from several hundred miles away. El is a very healthy kitty to this day. It is nice to have friends like that.

While I don't mind taking some risk in sharing my truth, I have to realize that I do not have the right to jeopardize the safety of anyone else in the process. Unfortunately, this section will stay a bit vague until either it is safe for her to come out openly, or until she leaves the planet. At the time of this writing, which was about a year after first meeting, she had gone into hiding for some reason, with only a message that she had to move and would not be communicating.

While it is safer for her if I don't know her location, it is also heart-breaking that we can't relate more openly. That is such a shame, not only for those of us who knew and loved her, but also for humanity as a whole. It is a tremendous added incentive for me to work harder toward making this world a safe place for our galactic cousins to visit openly.

One of the last messages I received from Tashina when she was previewing my work on the book was this: "You have put it in a way people can understand—very accurate and tasteful. The hope is many will read and apply what is there—Keep up the great work—You are a bridge between worlds—Namasté"

CHAPTER EXERCISE: CLASH OF CULTURES

Over the ensuing months since first meeting Tashina, my relationship with this visitor had its ups and downs. My tendencies to be open and want to share, and her desire to lead a relatively reclusive life to protect her safety, have clashed. I wanted to introduce her to some of my friends without revealing who she truly was, but in retrospect some of that was that sneaky ego creeping in and enjoying the secret, and that was wrong of me. Also, I would take things pretty literally and at face value and misinterpret when she was saying things to be polite. She had of course started with her cover story, and later moved into the truth, but it became hard to know for sure what was real and what was still cover story or politeness. There were some confusions of culture, and I still have not totally figured out how to relate to this higher dimensional being. It is not as easy as you might think at first, especially under the conditions of secrecy that constrained us.

So your chapter exercise is to imagine yourself suddenly transported into a totally different culture, the Bushmen of the Kalahari or the Australian Aborigines or nomadic Mongolian Herders, for example, and trying to relate to and get along in their culture. Imagine the social *faux pas* that you might commit out of ignorance of their ways. Take some time to really think about this, and then, if possible, find ways to interact with different cultures. You don't necessarily have to travel to distant lands. You can partake in cultural events closer to home, whether it is Cinco de Mayo celebrations, Japanese Obon Festivals, Falun Gong (Falun Dafa) http://www.faluninfo.net/ or whatever else is going on in your area. You can also practice by simply visiting a Himalayan or other ethnic Restaurant and getting to know the staff and a few of their native words and customs. Go in with the intent to learn about them and what of their culture you might incorporate into your own life. Respect them and their culture and sincerely desire to expand your understanding of their way of life, and they will respect you for the effort.

Now kick it up another notch. Do the basic Oneness meditation, and then imagine you are selected as an initial contactee when open First Contact starts to occur. Your "job" is to act as an intermediary between our Star Cousins and the citizens of Earth, to help smooth the introductions, allay fears, and explain what is going on to a public that is of widely varied opinions on the subject. Some people have been having their own contact, at least at a consciousness level, for some time. Others have been indoctrinated though fear and superstition that ETs are agents of the Devil, and are thus very fearful and suspicious of the visitors. You will run into everything in between these extremes as you try to work toward a safe and peaceful First Contact for the peoples of Earth.

Consider that we don't even have religious tolerance or good relations between our own cultures right now, so you can start to under-stand how daunting the task is going to be to introduce a very different culture to the rest of us. First Contact will most likely be with ET cultures that look very much like us, as they too are aware of the cultural hurdles we have to surmount. We may learn that we are actually descendants of colonists from some of these worlds, and having a genetic connection will help ease the early stages of interaction. Later, as we grow in our acceptance, we will probably start to meet others who may be significantly different from us physically, but if we are ready we can still find common ground and acceptance, and in this way expand our world (cosmic) view even more.

"TALKING" WITH ET

What is it like to talk with an ET? Maybe the thought never crossed your mind, though hopefully reading this book has led you to put yourself in that place or to imagine yourself doing something similar to what I have experienced. Hopefully you have given some thought as to how you would go about your own first contact. I can also assure you that if you have put out the intention to work with ethical extraterrestrial entities in a mutually respectful relationship, they will rejoice at the invitation. Also know that they will not give it to you faster than you can take it, which may seem painfully slow to you, but a pace that they may deem appropriate for you so that you don't "Explode!" **"First of all, do no harm"** seems to be their motto. So, if it is not happening fast enough for you, then work on yourself and see what *your* mental blocks might be.

Talking may, in fact, be a rather poor term, as my contacts for the first nine years were entirely non-verbal. I would receive mostly very distinct emotions or I would get spurts of creativity and start transcribing a poem or a discourse, and it was apparent that the inspiration for the message was from somewhere else. So, don't expect your first contact to be a verbal conversation with a physical being, as that would probably be too much for most people to handle right off the bat. Instead, be perceptive of your impressions and intuitions, especially when meditating or in the hypnogogic borderline sleep state, and most especially if you have been putting out the intention that you desire contact.

Most contact that is happening right now is probably in the Lucid Dream state or deeper states where you may not remember any of it consciously. In fact, many of you reading this book probably have already agreed to be light workers on a soul contract level, and are quite likely going to night school right now and don't even know it. Many are being trained for the coming changes on our planet and within our societies, and that training will rise into consciousness at the appropriate time. You might have glimpses of this subconscious training in your dreams or as you meditate and prepare yourself for potential contact. As things evolve, and especially if you ask, they will probably let more of your experiences bubble to the surface as rapidly as you are ready for them.

The best advice I have is to enjoy the journey, and to know that you are not going insane. As Bashar[54] says, as you travel this path, "sometimes you will feel you are going crazy, but this kind of crazy is a good thing, crazy will save you." This paraphrases a saying I have had for many years that "you have to be a little bit crazy to keep from going insane." It was nice to have Bashar back me up on that account. I guess the common ground between the two statements is that to experience the larger realities does not make you insane; *DENIAL* of what you have experienced is what will make you insane.

So, early contact will likely be rather subtle, but if you persist, engage in serious introspection of your motives and reactions, and desire to move forward for the right reasons, very interesting things can start to happen. You might just start to connect with some very interesting people through interesting synchronicities. If you have refined your soul to the point where you are trustworthy and not going to spill the beans to make your fortune from the story at others' expense, you might just find that one of your new friends is actually one of the million or so ETs living among us right now. (According to Tashina and other sources.) If you are fortunate enough to be taken into their confidence as a "Friendly," you can be in for a truly life-changing experience. Your world can suddenly get a whole lot bigger, and at the same time you allow the visitor a chance to "Let their Hair Down" in a safe environment. This can be as healing for them as it is enlightening for you, and your insights may also help them to get along in our world, especially if they are relatively new here.

Imagine life from their perspective, living a secret life and a cover story, no birth certificate or other related documentation, difficulty getting a passport, big holes in their résumé, and worried that the wrong people might discover them. The doctor might report physiological anomalies they discovered to higher authorities like medical societies or even NASA. Perhaps they are even trying to raise a family on this hostile planet, just put yourself in that place if you will.

This is kind of like the double life of an illegal alien from a foreign country who is trying to get by while concealing their true identity, only in this case it is a double life on steroids. Also, understand that many of them come from higher "Dimension" worlds, and that they have to lower their vibrations significantly in order to take on a 3rd dimensional

---

54   www.bashar.org

physical body, holding their metaphorical nose as they sink into the cesspool of humanity. Furthermore, they become just as vulnerable as you or I when they take on physical form, for they are generally not able to get rapid assistance if needed, and thus they can feel very isolated. I have found that the ones living amongst us are not as omnipotent as I had once believed, but are very much mortal. They even have some similar fears, especially concerning what might happen to them if they were discovered by the wrong people. This may be a bit new to them, for where they come from fear is not a common emotion. If they have a family here, then their fears are probably more toward the safety of the family, especially the innocent defenseless children who may not even understand that they are different.

They very much desire the opportunity to speak openly with someone and to share what they know with humans who are ready to handle it. If you are ready and have properly prepared yourself, the floodgates can open up for you in very interesting ways. Just know that if you are after their technology so that you can get an exclusive patent on food replicators for the whole planet and become a gazillionaire, it probably isn't going to happen! They will share with you what you will use unselfishly to help humanity and the planet, but selfish goals will shut things down instantly. Being disciplined in your thinking and honest with yourself can be a great advantage here.

Why would someone leave a peaceful, cooperative, love and gratitude-based world to come on assignment to Earth? They do this for the same reasons some of us work in the worst of slums in the poorest of countries, for a love of humanity. It is very much like a Peace Corps volunteer or teacher volunteering to work in some poor corner of the world out of an altruistic desire to help the people improve their lives and an opportunity to help them grow and evolve. Respect them for the sacrifice they have made, and give them your gratitude. Someday in the not too distant future, humanity will be moving out among the stars, and we will be in a similar role of helping other emerging societies. Learn what you can from this side of the experience so that you can apply it from the other side when you get the opportunity, if not in this lifetime then in another.

So let's look at the conversation from their side as to what it is like talking with us. No matter how advanced we are, it is a bit like us going down to skid row, talking to the drunks, and trying to have an intelligent philosophical conversation about the newest theories in quantum physics. It probably isn't going to go too far, and the company could be rather uncomfortable to be around, especially if they are suspicious of your motives. You have to make a distinguished effort to lift yourself above the baseline and show that you are trying to meet our Extraterrestrial neighbors halfway. When you do, they WILL notice, as I learned by personal experience!

CHAPTER EXERCISE: WHAT WOULD YOU SAY?

Take some time and think about what you would say and how you would react if you found yourself talking to one of our visitors, especially one who was living among us.

Take more time, and think it through even more deeply, as this is not something that you can pass over superficially. The deeper you contemplate and role-play, the more prepared you will become. Really try to get into it.

I'll wait!

Now, go back over your thoughts and see if the Ego was engaged?

Even though you may have been found worthy of initial contact, the unchecked human ego, which runs most of our lives, can sabotage many good efforts. I have seen it dilute the effectiveness of many in the UFO community, as ego-created superiority leads to turf battles and discord. Instead we should all be working together to find the answers that help us evolve into the higher consciousness that both precedes and accompanies open contact.

RANDOM THOUGHTS ABOUT RANDOM THOUGHTS

Back in 1999 I did some thinking about how to best prepare people for Extraterrestrial Contact, and did a thought experiment on the subject. It evolved into a policy suggestion for Project Starlight. Here is that paper as I wrote it then.

Random Thoughts about Random Thoughts
Telepathy, the Universal Translator—and how it will Change Society.

Te*lep*a*thy: communication from one mind to another by extrasensory means.

While meditating on some new aspects of the meaning of life, I felt the topic of how telepathy might change society was worthy of a *thought experiment* in the tradition of the Greek Philosophers of old. From that starting point, here are my Random Thoughts on Telepathy.

Before we can properly consider how telepathy may change society, we need to have a basis for where we are now. Telepathy is currently dismissed or even ridiculed by most people, if they give it any thought at all. Most of the people who do consider the subject think of telepathy as either a special gift you are endowed with at birth, an occult or even evil power, or just a myth that is not really true. Study of the subject is not encouraged by government grants or national initiatives.

Society itself thinks little of the subject of telepathic abilities, and while there is some discussion of body language and other methods to detect deception, about the closest most people get to telepathy is an intuitive sense that something doesn't ring true. As a result, we live in a society full of hidden agendas, ulterior motives, and outright deception. Politicians have raised this to an art form, telling us a plausible reason for something; while the real reasons for whatever they are doing lays behind the scenes hidden in political favors and campaign contribution paybacks. Some large companies have also become very adept at the art of the political maneuver. They contribute to both candidates, and then

when either candidate wins, they call in their debts and get the government to force us to buy something that they can't sell to us on its own
merits.

We live in a world where very little is truly honest and can be taken
at face value. We even consider it OK to tell little white lies to avoid
hurting someone's feelings. This is the normal way of life for most
people. As a child I had trouble fitting in well socially, mostly because I
was honest and said what I was thinking. I did not filter my thoughts
before speaking. This may be where we are headed as we learn to use
telepathy more easily in society, and it will require a shift in thinking as
we adjust to the new honesty this imposes.

Currently, most people are very sloppy in their thinking, and believe
all that matters is what they say or what they do. As more and more
people learn that Telepathy is relatively easy and can be learned to at
least basic proficiency within just a few days, others will discover that
their motives will become ever more transparent. They will have to
become more disciplined in their thinking, and even examine their own
motives very carefully. Any hidden motives will become more apparent
to others, even if not fully known to themselves. While I don't think
telepathy will replace spoken language completely, at least overnight, I
think it will temper what is spoken as more people become increasingly
proficient at getting underlying impressions of what other people are
really thinking. You will have to say what you are thinking, and think
with discipline, since any discrepancy will be readily apparent to anyone
proficient in Telepathy.

What effect will this have on society? I am hopeful that as lies and
deception become more transparent it will lead to a more open and
honest way of dealing with everything from business and politics to
personal relations. Thinking "Look at Joe, he is such a conceited, self-
centered jerk, but he can get me that promotion" and then saying, "Hi,
Joe, you look great, nice suit!" is not going to cut it anymore (unless Joe
is the type who may not get it, even if someone spelled it out to him in
plain language). If private thoughts and motives can no longer be
hidden, we will have to become more careful about what we think, and
this should lead to better self-discipline.

While working on some rudimentary attempts at telepathic
communications with non-human entities this summer, I went in with the
understanding that my life and my motives were an open book to those
I was trying to communicate with. It appeared probable that they would
have a much higher level of skill in this area, not necessarily because
they are born with superior abilities, but more likely because it is

accepted and fostered as a normal skill for them. Knowing that they would probably know more about me than I know about myself, I had to examine my own concepts and motives more closely than ever before. While there is some concern that you are losing privacy, I found that if I went in with a pure heart and honest intentions, I had nothing to fear, and that it did not feel invasive at all. Anyone who is used to hiding their true thoughts and saying what they think will give them the best advantage will probably find this new means of communication threatening. Anyone who lives honestly and openly will adapt with very little effort. I think the incentive will be for society to move toward increasing honesty, with far reaching but hopefully positive implications.

Let's consider these areas:

Personal communications:

We have already touched on this a bit, but it would extend a lot further. Currently, any mention of telepathic abilities or impressions is generally dismissed by our society, and we are discouraged rather than encouraged from developing these abilities. I think we actually use telepathy more than we realize.

Starting in the earliest stages of development, I suspect that babies get a lot of their impressions from their parents through telepathy, as well as body language. In our society, they soon learn to associate words with impressions and objects, and language develops. This is an imperfect process, and few realize how differently different people interpret the same words and phrases. This is especially true of written words where there is no associated body language or vocal inflections to temper the meaning.

As we grow older and start to develop romantic relationships, we again go through a period where telepathic abilities seem to naturally occur in spite of our culture. Think back to when you were first in love. How often did you finish the other person's sentence, answer the phone before it rang because you were thinking about calling your love and they were already in the process of calling you, or just "know" what the other person was thinking. In most honest love relationships, I think this is the way it works, at least at first. Over time, as the relationship settles in, I think most people return to a more "normal" way of relating. If our culture understood and supported these telepathic abilities as NORMAL, I think we could keep that exciting feeling of closeness and mutual honesty for the rest of our lives. It is said that many twins have this special link throughout their lives, knowing what the other is thinking or when they are hurt or in trouble, and it is considered normal or at least accepted for them. Why not for the rest of us?

I call telepathy the universal translator because, at the core level, we think in terms of objects, symbols, and concepts. This is the level on which telepathy works. We then translate these symbols into spoken language. This telepathic aspect of pure communication will help level the playing field and allow a better exchange of ideas and concepts not only across different languages and cultures, but also different races and species.

Business relationships:

Ever wonder what the person across the negotiating table was really thinking? How would it affect the negotiations if you knew? Furthermore, how would it affect negotiations if they also knew what you were thinking and what your motives were? Labor negotiations, merger talks, business deals, sales calls, and virtually every other aspect of business would change dramatically. I think the "Us versus Them" mentality would have to fade, and a healthier basis of mutual benefit would have to develop. Negotiations on all levels would have to be more open and honest. Truly honest business practices do survive right now, but often get drowned out in the sea of deception all around them. As we move into the age of Telepathic ability, those who run their business from a basis of honesty would begin to enjoy the advantage that they should have now. This is as it should be. They will be recognized for what they are, and all the others will have to improve their way of doing things if they want to keep up.

Telepathy will thus not only "promote" the motivation of cooperation over the heretofore motive of competition, it will most likely IMPOSE it. The result would then become "win-win" cooperative/competition business relationships and transactions. It would spell the end of the old cut-throat, back-stab your way to the top business model, and promote the transition to a model where the honest decent guy does win and get ahead. I for one think this would be a giant step forward.

Politics:

Where do I start? In Plato's time politicians who said what they thought the people wanted to hear, and then creatively reinterpreted it to do whatever they wanted to do were referred to a Sophist, and they were much despised by the philosophers. This is the way it still is in many political and corporate settings. Little has changed in 2600 years!

Webster's defines **Soph*ist:** as expert, wise man, to become wise, to **deceive**. 1. Any of a class of ancient Greek teachers of rhetoric, philosophy, and the art of successful living prominent about the middle of the 5th century B.C. for their adroit subtle and allegedly often specious reasoning. 2. A captious or fallacious reasoner.

Soph*ism is further defined as an argument apparently correct in form but actually invalid, *esp.* such an argument used to deceive.

These concepts carry over into the definitions of sophisticated and sophistication. Check them out for yourselves.

While Plato railed against these deceptions and pled for honesty with others and with self, it is clear to anyone with discerning reasoning that his concept for how things ought to be did not capture the mainstream of politics. The truly honest and honorable politician is a rare bird in any era. Perhaps the Sophist of the ages discouraged the development of natural abilities like telepathy and intuition simply because these abilities would allow most people to see through their political deceptions. Perhaps they were just too lazy and undisciplined in their own thinking, and did not want to have to rise to a higher standard. In any event, I believe the nurturing of our natural abilities will lead to a massive change in the way governments do business around the world, and I think it will be a change for the better. Imagine honesty in government and decisions based on the best interest of the people. **What an enlightened concept!**

I think Dr. Steven Greer has done an excellent job of thinking about the social, business, and political aspects of the disclosure of the reality of Extraterrestrial contact. Spending a week with him in Crestone really enlightened me as to why all of this change has to be done carefully, and not like a bull in a china shop. Change is often resisted and seldom fully understood by most. They are comfortable with the status quo, even if it is not the best for them, since it is what they know and somewhat understand. Change is uncomfortable to most, but in change there is great opportunity for improvement. Please read Dr. Greer's excellent paper on the "Implications of an Extraterrestrial Disclosure.[55]" What I have attempted to do here is use the same type of reasoning and then apply it to the "Implications of Large Numbers of Citizens developing our Natural Telepathic Abilities"! While I have only scratched the surface of this topic, I hope it has given you pause to reflect.

A recent Roper Poll commissioned by the National Institute for

---

[55] http://www.cseti.org/position/greer/csetibrf.htm and
http://www.disclosureproject.org/docgallery.shtml

Discovery Science offers some hope. Only 2.3% of those polled felt an announcement of the discovery of advanced extraterrestrial life would cause a major change in their lifestyle (leave job, take up arms, hide in hills) and only 3.8% said they would take up weapons and hide if ET craft were headed toward Earth (surprisingly, only 0.3% said they would contact their clergy for advice). Only 1.1% said they would be "Very frightened" if ETs looked very different from humans, 78% said they were personally psychologically fully prepared to handle the evidence of advanced extraterrestrial life.

Relating specifically to the issue of Telepathy, 63.5% said that if they were shown that ETs had just landed and could communicate telepathically with humans, they would be ready and willing to learn this new skill and another 14% would be somewhat interested. 7.7% would be disbelieving, 13% would be somewhat nervous, and only 1.8% would be terrified.

Those of us with any experience in CSETI already know the preceding premise is true, that ETs have landed and communicate telepathically with humans. Many of us know this through personal experience. Others can debunk all they want; they cannot change what we KNOW! It is my suggestion that wrapped into the Project Starlight disclosure effort be a consideration of the points I have made above. I suggest that possibly efforts be made in parallel to expand people's awareness of consciousness and the development of their own natural abilities, even before the rest of the disclosure comes about. This will help ease the transition when the time comes. I am very aware that while you can lead a horse to water, you can't make them drink. However, the science of consciousness is becoming more accepted, and is perhaps worthy of support in areas that are mutually beneficial. As people become more aware of the possibilities, acceptance and change will come more easily. I see the world moving in the right direction, slowly and with resistance, but also with great slow inertia! I am hopeful for a better world for my kids and their kids, and so on. As pioneers in this social and diplomatic effort, our jobs will not be easy, but they will be rewarding. When you find those who are ready for greater possibilities, gently nudge them in the right direction. Slowly, gradually, we can raise the consciousness of the entire planet to a level where all things are possible!

Visualize the world you want to create, a better world for all our future generations. It is a goal worthy of our humble efforts. Listen to your inner voice and do what you can to bring it about. Keep your eye on the goal, but just as importantly, **Enjoy the Journey!**

CHAPTER EXERCISE: TELEPATHY

This one is going to be more free form for you. Devise your own simple telepathy experiments. Perhaps have a friend thought-project something to you. It might be a picture they are looking at, an object, a simple line drawing, or projecting an emotion. You could use a set of four cards (make sure you understand the concepts of probability, in university experiments the hit rate was very little above chance). See if you can pick it up. Your friend should be out of your view so as to not unconsciously give you subtle body language clues. Seated behind you would be fine.

Practice for fifteen minutes to half an hour for several days, reversing rolls at times. See how it goes. You might also review events in your life where telepathy might have been an element of what happened. With the understanding you have now, you might just find you have been using telepathy subconsciously more than you previously realized. Have fun with it and don't get discouraged if you don't get every try right.

WHAT ARE THEY WAITING FOR?

In a nutshell, I think **they are waiting for us to Grow Up!** Can I put it any more succinctly?

Think about it; is humanity ready for open contact with our neighbors? We are easily manipulated by our leaders to think that anyone different from us is a threat. In fact, before any war our "leaders" work to create the perception that the "enemy" is not only different, but somehow Sub-Human! They will point out some physical characteristic that is different, such as a distinctive nose, skin color, or a distinctive article of cultural dress. They will then promote some derogatory name for the group, such as Japs, Krauts, Ragheads, Infidels, and such in order to de-humanize the "enemy" in the minds of their own people and their own soldiers, thus making it easier to convince them of the "necessity" of killing the enemy.

Just writing the derogatory words above sears my soul, it is so distasteful to me. I know many wonderful people from all of these cultures. I included them only in the hopes that it will trigger some serious introspection on your part as to how you may have allowed yourself to be manipulated in your thinking about others in the past.

German prison guards at the concentration camps, when asked if they had any remorse at killing the defenseless Jews, were often confused by the question. They had been so thoroughly conditioned that their prisoners were not humans that they did not have human emotions toward exterminating them. It was more like shooting rabbits that were overrunning your farm fields to them. We as a world civilization need to wake up to this and never allow ourselves to participate in anything similar in the future.

Do not be too hard on yourself if you find yourself to have been lacking relative to your current insight. The techniques were very carefully thought out Psychological Warfare principles applied against a citizenry and its soldiers to get them in a frame of mind to accept something they would not under other circumstances consider doing. If you simply start to understand how this manipulation of the mass psyche works, and are able to recognize it when you see it in the future, then we have all made great progress towards bringing peace to our world.

Another example of why not all of us are ready to meet our cosmic neighbors is religious indoctrination. Acceptance of peoples from other places and other dimensions varies a lot among religions and belief systems. Native Americans have long had a relationship with the star people, while on the other extreme one major televangelist is on record as saying that UFOs and ETs are agents of the Devil. Even simply having seen them meant that YOU were in league with the Devil, and he added that it was a "Good" Christian's duty to "Stone that person (you) to Death"!

Talk about psychological manipulation! Do you think any member of that flock is going to report a UFO/ET encounter? Not likely! In fact, they may even doubt the experience themselves, deny it internally, or simply filter it out and not register it at a conscious level at all. If you thought the psychological pressure to remain quiet and keep a UFO/ET encounter inside was tough on pilots, imagine how it must be among these religious fundamentalists, especially if the majority of them actually buy into that belief system about our visitors being agents of the Devil.

While most people would pull up short of stoning someone to death (murder), there is probably a core group who believe that every word this televangelist speaks is the direct word of God, and would feel it their duty, **in the name of God,** to commit a very un-Godlike act. So, if I am considered to be in league with the Devil for having had UFO/ET encounters, then an ET who was living among us who made themself known as such would be in even worse jeopardy. We laugh at primitive superstitions, and even the irrationality of the Inquisition or the Salem Witch Trials (not that long ago in our history), and yet how many of us recognize the same kind of thinking and manipulation going on today?

Are we grown up enough to interact with significantly different peoples and cultures in a mature manner? Think about it! Just as Peace must begin with YOU, so must the change in our attitudes concerning our cosmic neighbors. As you become clear in your own attitudes, and find the courage to express them in conversation with others, you will be planting seeds of acceptance among our culture. You will also be paving the way towards that day when there is wide enough acceptance that we can meet our neighbors openly and safely, see ourselves from a much bigger perspective, and learn our true place in the grand scheme of things.

The following poem I wrote in about a half an hour in a poetry workshop, and later submitted to Yoko Ono when she asked for Peace submissions to be enshrined in her Imagine Peace Tower in Reykjavik, Iceland. A reply was received from Yoko, thanking me for the Peace Poem and informing me that it would indeed be enshrined within the Imagine Peace Tower for all time. Pretty cool!

PEACE

Peace is much more than the absence of war,
indeed, peace involves letting your spirits soar.
Others may march to a different beat,
but they all walk with the same kind of feet.

Peace is simply seeing all humanity as one,
in this way life is so much more fun.
To know that we are all quite the same
makes meeting each other a very nice game.

Peace is selflessly helping each other,
just as if they were our brother.
Peoples from around the universe,
can all relate to this simple verse.

If we are truly of an open mind,
it is amazing the friends we will find.
Then we can learn from our differences,
and build bridges instead of fences.

Don Daniels © 2007

CHAPTER EXERCISE: SEE OURSELVES THROUGH THEIR EYES

Try this little thought exercise; Do the basic Oneness meditation, understanding that we are all awake and aware and conscious in the same manner, sparked by the same creative force, and thus intimately connected to all other conscious entities around the multiverse. Then imagine yourself as an extraterrestrial anthropologist, orbiting a few hundred miles above our planet, observing Earth civilization much as Jane Goodall observed chimpanzee culture. Imagine that you have the perspective of not just hundreds but thousands of years of Earth history.

Your goal is to determine if Earth is ready for "First Contact" or more precisely Open Contact with our larger family. Are we as a world ready to accept our visitors peacefully and without prejudice, or would we react with psychologically damaging worship and co-dependency, or even worse, abject fear?

I think that you will find that we are not quite there yet, so now ponder upon what you think we as a society and as a world civilization need to work on in order to become ready. Then contemplate how you might be able to help move us as a whole gently in that direction.

Last, put yourself in the position of one of the million or so ETs currently living among us on the surface. Your mission is to blend in, observe, and give gentle nudges to help individuals and humanity evolve to our true potential, to the point where we can become Galactic Citizens taking our proper and equal place at the galactic conference table. Simply spend some time meditating and contemplating the implications of this, and how you would go about your assignment. Imagine the emotions as you try to work among these sometimes hostile peoples, and how truly isolated you would feel at times.

If this is a little too much of a stretch at the moment; then imagine yourself as a human trying to blend in and observe on a different hostile world, or even imagine yourself as a spy in a foreign land for a first step. This will give you a glimpse as to what it is like for the advanced contact teams that are working among us here on Earth, and for the most part with the highest of ethics.

SERVICE TO SELF, SERVICE TO OTHERS, SERVICE TO THE UNIVERSE

I wrote this discourse/discussion for a mystical weekend retreat in 2009, with the intent of stimulating some spirited discussion. At that the topic was very successful, there were many ideas put forth, and greater insight gained by all. This is not in the form of a standard discourse, but instead mostly in outline form.

I will post this chapter on my website and suggest you use it more as a worksheet than a passive read. Print it out, make your own notes and modifications, contemplate your own answers, and then organize a group discussion of your own using your modified outline. The results may be quite enlightening not only for your friends, but just as much for you as you gain additional perspectives from the others in your group. I may or may not post the audio of our discussion group; permission will have to be gained from all, with the possible redaction of individual's names.

Discourse follows:

SERVICE TO SELF, SERVICE TO OTHERS, SERVICE TO THE UNIVERSE

While preparing for this topic, it seems helpful to define what Service is. According to the Encarta Dictionary:

ser·vice [súrvess] *noun* (*plural* **ser·vic·es**)

1. work done for somebody else: work done by somebody for somebody else as a job, duty, punishment, or favor
┃┃ *After 25 years of service to the company, all I got was a watch.*

2. helpful action: an action done to help somebody or as a favor to somebody
┃┃ *Would you do me one small service?*

3. **work for customers:** work done for the customers of a store, restaurant, hotel, or similar establishment, often with regard to whether it pleases them or not

    I I *The service in this restaurant is lousy.*

    I I *You can never get any service in this place!*

4. **house servant's work:** work done as a servant in a private house

5. **use:** the use that can be had from a machine or piece of equipment

    I I *Treat it carefully, and it'll give you years of good service.*

6. **use or operation:** current use or operation

    I I *The number you have dialed is not in service at this time.*

7. mechanical engineering **maintenance of machinery:** the act of cleaning, checking, adjusting, or making minor repairs to a piece of machinery, especially a motor vehicle, to make sure that it works properly

    I I *take the car in for a service*

8. **meeting of public need:** a system or organization that provides people with something that they need, e.g. public transportation or a utility

    I I *the tourist information service*

    I I *a bus service*

9. **government agency:** a body of people who carry out work for the public benefit within an organization run by local or national government

    I I *the diplomatic service*

    I I *the police service*

10. **one of armed forces:** the armed forces of a country, or one of its branches

    I I *Which branch of the service is your daughter in?*

11. **form of public worship:** a religious ceremony usually involving specific forms for worship and prayer

    I I a memorial service

12. religion **religious ritual:** the prescribed form for a particular act of public worship or religious ceremony

❘ ❘ *the marriage service*

13. set of dishes: a set of dishes and cups for use in serving a particular meal

❘ ❘ *dinner service*

14. racket games: Tennis Service

15. serving of legal document to somebody: the delivery of a legal document   such as a writ or summons

plural noun

1. skills and work: the work that somebody can do or does by virtue of their job, profession, or training

❘ ❘ *You seem to need the services of a plumber.*

❘ ❘ *I'm afraid we've decided to dispense with your services.*

2. work that does not make anything: jobs and businesses that provide something for other people but do not produce tangible goods, e.g. banking and insurance

3. things provided by government: things that are provided by national or local government and paid for by taxation, e.g. education, health care, and roads

4. facilities for travelers: facilities for travelers available at intervals along a highway, e.g. stores, restaurants, toilets, and a service station

❘ ❘ *There are no services at the next exit.*

transitive verb (past and past participle **ser·viced**, *present participle* **ser·vic·ing**, *3rd person present singular* **ser·vic·es**)

1. provide something for community: to provide a community or organization with something that it needs

❘ ❘ *The electric company services all nine counties.*

3. pay interest on debt: to pay interest on a debt

adjective

1. providing service not goods: relating to jobs or businesses that provide services but do not manufacture goods

3. used by employees or for deliveries: intended for employees or deliveries rather than for members of the public (*often used before a noun*)

| | *a service elevator*

[Pre-12th century. Via French < Latin servitium *"servitude"* < **servus** *"slave"*]

-ser·vic·er, *noun*

press somebody *or* **something into service** to use something or somebody for an unusual purpose, especially in an emergency situation

Microsoft® Encarta® 2008.
© 1993-2007 Microsoft Corporation. All rights reserved.

Whew! Those definitions cover a lot of ground, but let's consider focusing more on the topic of this discussion, how people focus their efforts, whether mostly for their own benefit, for the benefit of others, or for the benefit of humanity, the world, or the universe.

As I developed this topic it became apparent to me that the difference between service to self and service to the multiverse is more of a continuum than a set of fixed, well defined groupings, so let's examine this just a bit as we work our way up the continuum.

Pure service to self is the person whose every action is to enrich themselves or enhance their power or status purely at the expense of others. This goes so completely against the Mystical grain that it is not worth spending much time or effort on, we know it when we see it and we know that Karma will balance the scales in time, so we just avoid that paradigm and don't give it energy.

From the Rosicrucian Positio[56]: "*Concerning human relationships, we think that people are more and more self-seeking and leave less and less room for altruism. Of course, outbreaks of solidarity occur, although it happens only occasionally during such catastrophes as floods, storms, earthquakes, etc. In ordinary times, the policy of "everyone for oneself" predominates in behavioral patterns. In our view, this increase in individualism is again a consequence of the excessive materialism that is rampant today in modern societies. Nevertheless, the resultant isolation should eventually bring about the desire and need to renew contact with others. Moreover, we may hope that this solitude will lead everyone to go increasingly within and eventually become*

---

[56] http://rosicrucian.org/publications/positio.pdf

aware of spirituality."

Service to others is where most Mystics spend most of their time. It is difficult to be totally in service to others at all times, as unless you are independently wealthy it is generally necessary to make some income to support yourself and your family. So now I ask you how we can best balance service to others with taking care of our own needs? .....

Discussion:

Examples: Teachers, EMTs and Paramedics: Working to benefit others and receiving a paycheck (usually relatively small) for their service.

Question: Is service through an intermediary like a church or charitable organization really service to the Universe, or is it service to the organization?

.... *Take time to Discuss.*

The lines can get rather fuzzy. I think some church or charitable service, while well intentioned, is serving the particular church more than humanity, while nearer the far end of the spectrum someone like Mother Theresa, while connected to a church, served humanity without many, if any, strings attached.

Question: Was Mahatma Gandhi in service to his religion, to his people, or to Humanity?

How can we raise our sights to even higher levels? How can we be of **Service to the Universe?** *Discussion:*

Examples: The Dalai Lama and his worldwide educational programs. Yoko Ono and her **Imagine Peace Tower**[57].

There are many other efforts to uplift human thinking and bring about a spiritual evolution of humanity, such as the Peace Consciousness[58] project and other similar efforts.

In most cases these efforts provide no income, and must therefore be part-time endeavors in our current paradigm. The further up the spectrum you go, the more selfless are your efforts, and the more they are aimed at uplifting and evolving humanity as a whole. Other efforts may be focused on the environment of the planet, or at working toward better relations with other nations, or even with other civilizations from around the universe.

Discussion: Do humanity's actions have any effect on the rest of the universe?

---

[57] www.imagine**peace**tower.com

[58] www.PeaceConsciousness.org

Do we affect the cosmic field of consciousness?

Points: Fundamental oneness of all, quantum holographic interactions. Rogue planet status?

Question: What is the Multiverse? hypothetical cosmos of multiple universes: *a hypothetical cosmos that contains our universe as well as numerous other universes and space-times.* How can we use this concept to expand our thinking beyond 3rd dimensional physicality to include higher dimensional planes of existence?

Question: Where do we fit into this larger paradigm of existence, and do our actions affect higher planes and dimensions? Can we experience this through Out of Body travel to different planes?

Question: What is the difference between a Consensus Reality and a Thought Responsive reality, and is mental discipline more important in the higher realms?

Point: As we enter higher and more thought responsive realms, our THOUGHTS manifest much more rapidly. Is this true even of undisciplined random thoughts, and could that cause us considerable problems?

Question: How can we as individuals and as a society progress and evolve to higher levels of being?

Question: What are the advantages to us and to our world of working to expand our thinking to fit this larger paradigm?

From the Rosicrucian Positio: *Concerning humanity's relationship with the Universe, we believe that it is based upon interdependence. As children of the Earth, and as the Earth is a child of the universe, we are therefore children of the universe. The atoms composing the human body originate in nature and remain within the confines of the Cosmos, which causes astrophysicists to comment that "We are children of the stars." Even though we are indebted to the universe, it should also be noted that the universe owes much to humanity also—not its existence, of course, rather its reason for being. Indeed, what would the universe be if human eyes could not contemplate it? If our consciousness could not embrace it? If our soul could not be reflected in it? The universe and humanity need each other to know and even recognize each other, which reminds us of the famous saying: "Know thyself, and thou shalt know the Universe and the Gods."*

Nevertheless, we should not deduce that our conception of Creation is anthropocentric. Indeed, we do not make humans the center of the Divine Plan. Rather, let us say that we make humanity a focus of our concerns. In our opinion, humanity's presence on Earth is not the result of mere happenstance; rather, it is the consequence of an intention originating from a Universal

Intelligence commonly called "God." Although God is incomprehensible and unintelligible because of Transcendency, this is not true of the laws through which God manifests within Creation. As previously mentioned, we have the power—if not the responsibility—to study these laws and to apply them for our material and spiritual welfare. We even believe that in this study and application lie our reason for being, as well as our happiness.

Humanity's relationship with the universe also brings up the matter of knowing whether life exists elsewhere outside of Earth. We are convinced that this is the case. Since the universe includes approximately one hundred billion galaxies, and each galaxy has about one hundred billion stars, there probably exist millions of solar systems comparable to ours. Consequently, to think that only our planet is inhabited seems to us to be an absurdity and constitutes a form of egocentrism. Among the forms of life populating other worlds, some are probably more evolved than those existing on Earth; others may be less so. Yet they are all a part of the same Divine Plan and participate in Cosmic Evolution. As for knowing whether extraterrestrials are capable of contacting humanity, we feel that this will happen, and we are not spending time waiting for it. We have other priorities. Nonetheless, the day will come when this contact will happen, and it will constitute an unprecedented event. Indeed, the history of humanity will then integrate into that of Universal Life....RC

Closing thoughts: What can happen when we make ourselves available to be of service to the universe? .....

What if she asks a favor!

This can potentially become a very mutually rewarding relationship, if we are ready for it.

CHAPTER EXERCISE: LEAD YOUR OWN DISCUSSION GROUP

Your chapter exercise is to download this chapter file from the website www.EvolutionThroughContact.com and revise it to suit your own style. Write in your own answers to the questions and make your own examples for the various points. Then, get a group of friends together and have an evening of philosophical discourse. Everyone will learn from the process, both about human interaction and about themselves.

WHAT DO WE HAVE TO OFFER?

Many people are saying many things about why the ETs are interested in us, and perhaps somewhat less speculation as to what we have to offer them. Let me weigh in with some speculation on my part as to what feels more valid to me.

We are currently in a critical Post-Nuclear era[59] where we as a species have the ability and the technology to blow ourselves back into the Stone Age if not into extinction. Have we developed the spirituality and maturity to keep up with those very powerful technologies? Do you suppose this has ever happened before anywhere else in the universe? If you are still so anthropocentric as to think we are the only intelligent life in the universe, then just ask if this has ever happened anywhere on THIS planet at any time in our history!

If you do just a little digging, you will find accounts in the Vedic texts of great battles in the sky with flying shields and weapons that sound similar in description to atomic or nuclear bombs. There are also the legends of Atlantis and Lemuria. Lemuria was supposedly much longer ago and less well documented. Stories of the cause of Lemuria's demise are less clear, but Atlantis was supposedly destroyed by the greed and corruption of its leaders, and the misuse of advanced technology.

In the Christian Bible there is the account of Sodom and Gomorrah and the pillar of fire that destroyed those cities. That description of the pillar of fire strongly resembles a nuclear explosion of our time, and there have been discoveries of a material called Atomsite (which is sand fused into glass by an atomic explosion) in the Middle East, where there has never been a modern nuclear explosion.

Then there is the mystery of the statues on Easter Island that are glazed on

---

[59] Some say our Nuclear weapons rip the very fabric of the Multiverse, and affect other worlds as well as our own. If this is the case, it is an even stronger argument to remove the scourge of nuclear war from the face of the earth. Even if we think we have the right to destroy ourselves, do we have the right to destroy parallel universes?

one side as if they had been exposed to a nuclear explosion. These latter two examples have physical evidence in addition to legend or historical account.

Is it possible that our neighbors are watching us to see if we get it right this time? Is it like Jane Goodall studying the chimpanzees, or perhaps more accurately like anthropologists studying remote and isolated cultures around the world to learn more about ourselves as a species? Is it our cosmic cousins checking up on their descendants from the early colonies? Some say that they came here to live on this planet approximately 1.5 million years ago. If we are biological relatives to other star civilizations, it is logical that they would have an interest in our development. Did we lose track of our origins due to millennia of time or through deliberate distortions of our history by those who wanted to gain power and control over humanity?

David Wilcock[60] has uncovered science that clearly shows how DNA itself arises from a wave in the Source Field. There is very solid laboratory evidence that existing creatures can be transformed, in their embryonic state, from one species to another by nothing more than "wave genetics"—shining a laser that has the wave information from the DNA of another species into an embryo. This will be talked about in much greater detail in David's brand new book *The Source Field Investigations*.

David also says: "Once you get into the science you're going to see that the galaxy itself is responsible for writing the code of DNA and the human design is a galactic intelligent design."

WOW! Does that ever put a new spin on the old Creation/Evolution argument? Perhaps we are not so much direct BIOLOGICAL cousins of some of our neighbors, but perhaps we might be more created from the same blueprint carried on Photons around the universe! This too would help explain why so many of our visitors look quite similar to us. Obviously there are many possibilities to consider if we are willing to explore ideas outside the "official" history of humanity.

Then there are the spiritual explanations, the internet being rife with stories right now about how humanity is on the brink of ascension to a higher dimension or at least a more spiritual way of being. Stories abound about additional strands of DNA being activated in many of us by the photon belt or other means, or of *Junk* DNA becoming activated somehow. Some people claim first hand reports from a geneticist about just this thing being proven scientifically, but as of this moment I only have second-hand reports from credible witnesses, and no hard first-hand knowledge myself. Some people even predict that we will evolve to a full twelve-strand DNA to match the twelve chakras of

---

[60]   www.DivineCosmos.com

our evolving being, *Homo Luminous*.

In regards to our evolution I do see an increase in spiritual growth, even though it is not generally reported in the mainstream media. However, we must remember that one person's observations do not a scientific survey make, because you tend to attract around you people similar to yourself. Thus, as you grow spiritually, you will naturally see more spirituality in others.

Many people seem to be feeling more connected with each other and with our Earth now than ever before, and are thus becoming less inclined to play the part of a pawn in other people's manipulations or conflicts. There is even a new syndrome called variously Avatar Withdrawal, Avatar Blues, Avatar Depression, and Pandora Withdrawal, et cetera, related to the reactions some people have after watching the movie *Avatar*. People report that our world seems so dull, corrupt, and devoid of meaning compared to the way of life of the Na'Vi of Pandora. Perhaps people are seeing a better way of being, and are depressed because it seems so overwhelming to try to achieve that kind of spiritual connection on our corporate-controlled world. But if enough people truly want a more spiritual connection to our world and to each other, then it will start to manifest here, and in that way director James Cameron has allowed us to dream of a better way of being. That kind of movement is unstoppable even by governments, since it grows from the grass roots up.

Getting deeper into the spiritual aspects, some say that our freewill experiment into duality has taught us many lessons and thus has made us very powerful creators, and that our choices now will affect much more than just ourselves. Thus it is possible we are being observed and possibly even nudged to make good choices for ourselves, our galaxy, and possibly even our universe. That puts kind of a heavy responsibility on us to get it right, but we may have some help in the process, if we allow it. We should not consider any visitors as omnipotent gods who know it all; in some ways we have abilities they may never have dreamed of. We should take whatever wise council we may be able to get and combine it with our own intuition and wisdom, and in this way try to arrive at decisions that are beneficial to not only ourselves but also to all we share the universe with.

Some say that humans have the ability to manifest with only our minds, something we do at times without even realizing it and without making the connection to a thought we had at some time in the "past." Remember my friend, the one who manifested a new paint job for his pickup! He was able to make the connection since he was making a conscious effort and received a dramatic result. These same people say that most, if not all other peoples around our universe can manifest, but need the aid of technology. While I don't know if this is true, it is worthwhile to spend some time contemplating how we would handle our ability to manifest whatever we needed with a simple thought. Consider what kind of mental discipline would be necessary in order to avoid having stray or negative thoughts jump into form before we had a chance to think about the consequences. It might be wise to start practicing that kind of mental discipline right now; it will make the transition much easier. Spend some time thinking about how you could use these new abilities for the benefit of humanity and the universe.

At the very least we are a new technological society, starting to reach out into the universe, and they may have just a little parental concern that we are mature enough to use that technology wisely. They may also want to get to know us just as we would want to get to know a new neighbor.

CHAPTER EXERCISE: CONTRIBUTING TO THE UNIVERSE

Spend a little time thinking about how we might fit in with the rest of the universe and what we might be able to contribute as Galactic Citizens. Start with the basic Oneness meditation, and then contemplate what you might do and what you might want to contribute as we are introduced to the other civilizations we share this universe with. We are here on this schoolhouse planet in order to learn some very difficult but also very important lessons, and in the process to hopefully gain some wisdom. At the very least, we are learning how NOT to treat others. After we have moved into Galactic citizenship and learned how other societies are organized, then perhaps we can move out to other evolving worlds to help them evolve just as our star cousins are helping us right now.

Would you like to work on a ship monitoring a new civilization? Would you want to be more hands-on and be one of the ground troops living among them, blending in, observing them at close range, and even giving them gentle nudges or planting ideas to help keep them on a positive track? How would you deal with it if the planet you were working with was as violent and dysfunctional as Earth is now? Will you have learned your lessons well enough from Earth's transformation to be able to help them with theirs, or would you rather work with a more primitive but more peaceful world? If not in this lifetime, it is likely you will be in these roles in the near future, as that is a good part of why you are here at this time in Earth's development. Remember, you chose to be here, now the fun part is trying to remember why!

WHAT DO THEY HAVE TO OFFER US?

The most obvious answer is technology, but I'm not so sure that that is the only answer, or even the best answer. Sure, we could use their energy and transportation technologies, and it would help us quit polluting our planet to death, but there is much evidence that we already have many or most of those technologies within our covert projects (some given, some reverse engineered, and some developed by our own scientists). They have yet to see the light of day for the benefit of the public, for reasons of greed and power.

Open contact with our visitors would make it apparent to even Joe Six-pack that such advanced technologies exist, and would hopefully result in a lot of public clamor for our adoption of clean energy and transportation systems. This might force the hand of those who want to keep us on the fossil fuel paradigm. We might just create a stampede among them to be first to release those clean energy technologies that they have been hoarding, especially once it became apparent they were coming out anyway. So far, though, all we as a society seem to have demonstrated with any new technology has been to first use it to develop new and better ways of killing each other. Many years later it may start to filter down into advances that affect the general public in peaceful and beneficial ways. The best estimates are that the covert world is approximately 50 years ahead of what they let us have. When will that paradigm change?

An effect that I think will be even more paradigm changing than the new technologies will be a reassessment of our self-image in light of the news that we are not the only intelligent life in the universe. As we learn our true history and roots from those impartial observers and historians who have been watching our planet for millennia, we will have to re-examine a lot about ourselves. We will start to understand how deeply we have been deceived by those who write the history and control the news on this planet for their own gain. Once the truth is widely known and the deceptions exposed, we will be demanding new structures which have accountability to the people, and with this will evolve radically different ways of doing many things.

In fact, as we learn how civilizations around the universe handle the various structures of society, we will be in for some of the most revolutionary change this planet has seen in a very long time. Government, finance and business are in for a major overhaul once we learn of better ways of being. I suspect we will move back to more neighborhood and community-based organization for a while as we adapt. Old structures will fall and new, more fair and honest ones will be implemented. Then we can reach out again to form mutually beneficial business and trade relationships with others. It is my hope that empire and domination will give way to cooperation, mutual benefit, and respect, especially once it is known that our actions are being gauged to determine if we are ready to move out into the larger galactic family along with all that potentially has to offer. People will realize how childishly we have been behaving, and I would hope there will then be a desire and action by a critical mass of humanity to cause us to grow up and behave like the wonderful spiritual adults that we really are.

CHAPTER EXERCISE: NEW TECHNOLOGIES

Spend a little time thinking about how you would manage new technologies if they were given to you. Suppose you were one of the first to receive a free energy generator or an anti-gravity craft. Would you be able to use them strictly for the betterment of humanity, or would you still be tempted to use them to gain an advantage over others? If you have read this far, I seriously doubt that you are the type of person who would want to figure out a way to weaponize the technologies. It is my firm hope that humanity in general would be beyond that kind of thinking by the time this comes about. It is also quite likely that this kind of thinking is why they have not given us these technologies already. Do the basic Oneness meditation, and then spend a little time contemplating how you might help move humanity to the level where we are worthy of these kind of technologies. Remember that we are most effective when we lead by example.

Once worthy, consider what you would do if given new technologies. What types of things would you be most interested in having, and how would you use them to advance humanity?

HOW TO RELATE TO YOUR ET FRIENDS

First and foremost, relate to them as PEOPLE! Think of them as long lost cousins whom you are meeting for the first time, and you are catching up on each other's whole life experiences. You know nothing about what they have done all their life, just like if they had lived in foreign countries you have never visited. There is a lot to catch up on. But at the same time, don't pester them to death with a million questions. Often they just want to commune, to be together just to enjoy being together. Or they may just welcome a chance to let their hair down and speak openly in a safe environment. They may want to learn some things about you, to discuss philosophy, what your world view is, and how you plan to improve your world.

Above all, they want to be seen as equals, not as gods. If you worship their superior technology or insight, it can cause all kinds of problems, not the least of which is co-dependency. You can become dependent on them for answers or expect them to solve OUR world's problems, and that just messes up our initiative to fix our own problems. They know that our seeing them as gods or demi-gods can cause problems even for them, and it is quite possible that it has caused problems for both parties in our past history. Consider if the ancient Roman, Greek, Egyptian, Norse, Mayan, Incan, or other "gods" were actually cosmic visitors. Did that always go well for either party?

To make it easier for you to relate, imagine what it would be like if you, like the Connecticut Yankee, were transported back in time to one of these ancient civilizations, and were able to take your technology with you. How would you be treated? Would you want to be worshiped? Imagine if that is what happened. It would take a very balanced person to avoid having major ego problems from being treated as all wise, all knowing, all powerful. They could become co-dependent upon you to solve their problems, many of which you may not have the answers to. Do you wing it or do you try to explain that you are not omnipotent? What if they assume you are immortal? That could cause serious problems too.

Your being treated like a god could not only mess up their society, but also it could mess you up big time unless you were very balanced and grounded with your ego well in check. Turn the situation around and look at it from the perspective of our visitors. They understand this, and they want to avoid the traps that can harm both parties, including wanting to avoid creating a bad case of planetary co-dependency.

What do they want from a relationship with you? They want some preliminary contact with those individuals who are mentally balanced and psychologically prepared enough to relate to them appropriately, and who are willing to be of service to humanity as we move into more open contact. They want someone who can help educate others, at least those who are ready to hear, as to the truths of the situation and who can help lay the groundwork for a peaceful public "First Contact." They want people who can be leaders and educators when this event happens, and they want people with whom they can talk in order to gain further insight into the current state of humanity so that they can adjust their plans accordingly. They may also just want a friend with whom it is safe to simply relax and to talk openly about their perspective on humanity and the universe. If you have the balance and mental preparation to be that person, the world can become a VERY interesting place.

Here is a paper I wrote on the subject back in 2000. It still has many good points to ponder.

THE MOVIE STAR AND THE ET!

There is activity next door. The neighbor's house sold a couple of weeks ago, and now someone is moving in. Curious, you watch to see who it is, if they have any kids, etc. Much to your surprise, you recognize the new neighbors as some famous movie or music star; say Leonardo DiCaprio, Kate Winslet, Holly Hunter, Tom Cruise, Meg Ryan, or Shania Twain. Right now, you have two or more choices. Do you:

1.   Grab your camera and run next door to get a picture with your famous new neighbor so you can show it to all your friends, and possibly sell it and the info on where your new neighbor lives to the *National Inquirer*.

2.   Get together some homemade cookies and milk, and go over, introduce yourself and ask if there is any way you can help. Offer to grab a spare light bulb from your closet so they don't have to take time out to run to the store. Help carry stuff in.

Choice one may get you some fame, and possible money, from those who want to intrude on the private life of your neighbor, but it does not lead to a sustainable long-term relationship.

Choice two could be the start of a great friendship. Movie and music stars are assailed by fans seeking autographs all the time while at work. There are many people who want to make money or otherwise benefit from associating with them. There are also those who, out of jealousy or greed or ego, may want to harm your neighbor. If they bought the house next door, they want a quiet place to escape from all that. They are looking for a calm port in the storm. If you understand and respect that, you can become one of their closest and most respected friends.

Over the weeks and months, as your friendship grows, you find that you have more in common than you expected. You both want a quiet, safe place to raise your kids. You are concerned about what kind of world will be around several generations hence, and discuss ways you can help improve the outlook for future generations. You have ideas for improving the environment, and they are interested. You find ways you can work together and complement each other in truly unselfish ways to help achieve these mutual goals. Nobody outside your local neighborhood even knows they live there. You help protect their little sanctuary from the madness of the outside public world. They appreciate that, and recognize that as a friend you are *One in a Million!*

Over time, you accumulate some "family" snapshots from neighborhood cookouts, hikes in the mountains and such. These could be worth a lot of money if sold to the tabloids, but the thought never crosses your mind. Your friendship and relationship is worth much more than that.

Perhaps on the other side of you a great, though relatively unknown scientist/ inventor moves in. He is working on a free energy device that could change the world, and help end fossil fuel pollution. You network with your other neighbor and others you know, and help find quiet funding to complete the project. You know there are those who, due to greed or lust for power, do not want this project to succeed, and others who would want to turn it into weapons systems. So you help keep his project quiet, offering ideas and labor whenever you can. The long-term goals and the chance to improve life for all on this planet in the future are worth the effort now. You don't seek riches or glory, just the chance to help make a better future.

Then one day you are out camping with some friends. Watching the night sky, you see a smudgy streak that looks kind of like a meteor, but not quite. Then it stops abruptly and becomes a point of light, moving slowly toward you. As it gets closer, you can see a structured craft that does not look like anything you have seen before. RIGHT NOW, You have two or more choices. Do you:

1. Grab the camera and try to get that picture to sell to the *National Inquirer* for One Million dollars? Or,

2. Let them know that you would like to visit and get to know them better?

Ask if there is anything you can do to help them?

Choice two may take some courage! They may look like anything from tall blond Nordic people to small ape-like creatures to 6-foot Praying Mantis insect like creatures. They may not even be fully physical or look like any animal you have ever seen, but you are able to exchange thought impressions with them. You may have to overcome some past prejudices to give these visiting "People" the benefit of the doubt as you start this fledgling relationship. You are taking a personal risk in many ways, but you are also aware that there is tremendous potential for humanity if we can establish the proper type of relationship with these peoples. It must be a relationship that is based on trust, honesty and mutual respect. You elect to not even reach for the camera. You sense that your thoughts, intentions and motives are as transparent as water to your new guest. But strangely, you do not find this threatening at all as long as your motives are pure. It would only be a problem if you were trying to hide something.

You learn that over the years many humans have tried to take advantage of the ETs' early attempts to establish a relationship with us. Some have succumbed to greed or lust for power, some have taken technologies intended to heal our environment or heal our illnesses and turned them into weapons systems. Some people in power have known this for many years, but have kept us uninformed so that we would keep working to support our families and buy their gasoline and heating fuel and electricity.

About half of what we earn goes to taxes of one form or another, and much of that goes to building ever better weapons systems with which to destroy each other or anyone else who might drop by our planet for a visit. They do not allow us to know that in our galactic back yard we have neighbors who would like to get to know us better. We cannot get along with ourselves, let alone with others unlike ourselves. We fight wars and kill each other over minor differences in religion. We pollute our own planet almost beyond its ability to recover, and do not seem to care about what kind of mess we leave for future generations. Didn't we learn anything back in our sandbox days?

You learn and understand in a profound way that for at least the last 100 years or so, we have been *Humans Behaving Badly.* You want to make a difference, but it will take some time to figure out how. What can one person do? On the flip side, if one person puts their mind to it, what is there that they cannot do?

For now, you choose to just spend some time sharing ideas with your visitors, and letting a plan start to formulate. The quick buck from the photo or even the gazillion dollars for the rights to the new technologies you could get seems insignificant now compared with the potential for improving the future of humankind for many thousands of years to come. You have learned the lessons of friendship and trust from your neighbors. There is no amount of money that could cause you to betray them. This relationship you are just starting has the potential to last thousands or millions of years. What kind of value does that have?

During the course of the evening, you come to realize that your visitors and many others they associate with in the cosmic community want to see Earth advance, get its collective act together, and become worthy of joining in a larger intergalactic neighborhood. They will not come in and do it for us. They do not want us to be co-dependent. Instead, we must see the light and make the effort ourselves. Once we get started on the path, they will help us in many ways, but they want to be seen as neighbors, friends and equals, not as saviors or conquering heroes. This is going to be harder than you ever imagined, but then, maybe one person can change the world. Look what people like Buddha, Gandhi, Jesus, Baha'u'llah, and others accomplished in their short lifetimes. You will need some time to digest all these thoughts. You ask your visitors if you can meet again in a week or so. You get a favorable impression.

So many things are churning over in your head; you find it hard to sleep. Your whole life is about to change, and you are just beginning to realize some of the implications. Your very job, the career you worked so hard to train for, will soon be obsolete if you accomplish your goals. How will you provide for your family? Many people have a vested interest in not allowing you to get your message out. How will you deal with them and succeed, let alone survive? There are so many questions and only a few answers so far. What will you do?

What would **YOU** do? Would you disrupt your family and risk everything you have? How can you put a price on the cost to humanity if you don't succeed? Suddenly, your comfortable life becomes much less important, and all things take on a new perspective.

You remember the quote that *"Bad things happen when good people do nothing!"* Are you going to sit by the side and hope someone else does what is right, or will you step up and do it yourself?

Do YOU have the courage to do the right thing in a case like this? Not many people do. If you stand up and are counted, you will be "One in a Million" and one of the few who can lead this world into a brighter new millennium. Do you have what it takes?

© 2000 Don Daniels

CHAPTER EXERCISE: MEETING OTHER PEOPLES

For this chapter exercise, let's turn things around and look at it from the opposite perspective. Suppose you are part of a pre-contact team covertly visiting an emerging civilization on another planet. You would study the civilization and culture as much as possible from afar, or even from the vantage point of being cloaked and invisible to them. You might consult with higher dimensional beings that are guides and guardian angels to the people of that planet to get their perspective.

But eventually there comes the point where you move into places among them and interact with them directly. You come in perhaps as a traveler from another village to help explain why no one knows you. You make friends and find work in the community, preferably in some field that involves a lot of public contact. You will naturally make a few closer friends in the process. Do some serious contemplating on what attributes you would want among those you allowed closer friendships with, or even more important those you might take into your confidence.

Make a list, I'll wait!

......

Are you writing yet?

......

I'm betting that honesty, integrity and reliability were among your desired attributes, especially if you take a chance of being discovered. Personal integrity becomes even more important if you confide in some of these people, as you do not want them to turn around and betray you. How would their knowledge about you affect their Ego, and could they handle it? You might cross raging egos off the list of desired attributes. You are looking for someone who is balanced and stable. What other attributes did you consider desirable or undesirable?

Now take some time to meditate on these concepts even more deeply. Who could you trust? Think about your friends here on Earth and consider whom among them you could share a secret like this with if you were an Extraterrestrial visitor on this planet.

Scary thought, isn't it?

Now spend a little more time thinking about yourself, and contemplating if YOU are a person an Extraterrestrial would want to confide in. Don't expect perfection in yourself right away, but do take notes of areas you might want to work on.

TALKING ABOUT UFO/ET

If you share some of your experiences with friends (of maybe strangers at first, if that seems safer), you will most likely be surprised how common your experiences are. It is just that everyone has been conditioned to think that they are the only one who has had these experiences and are afraid to talk about them for fear others will think they are crazy. That stranger seated next to you on that four-hour flight can turn out to be an amazing therapist. You wouldn't believe some of the conversations I've had with passengers on commute flights going to and from work. Approach the subject of your experiences gently and feel them out and if they are receptive, then open up a bit. Often the flood-gates will open on the other side and they will just "ram dump" because you are the first person they could talk to about this strange experience they had sometime many years ago.

There is some safety in anonymity, and it is surprising how often this topic will blow wide open if you set the stage and offer a safe environment for them to share. This often entails your allowing yourself to be a little bit vulnerable, to let them know it is safe for them to share also, but I have ALMOST never been bit by that. In the one major case where I had some problems, it was partially a result of trying to deliberately make it safer for pilots to talk about the subject and I was pushing the envelope just a little bit, but on purpose. In the process I did make it a little more acceptable for pilots to talk about the subject, and also helped many of my fellow aviators by giving them an opportunity to tell their stories to me, often for the first time in their lives. I think it was well worth it.

CHAPTER EXERCISE: TALKING ABOUT
THE NEW PARADIGM

Find ways to discuss your thoughts and these new insights with your friends. In this way you can start to practice the role of diplomat. Understand that their reactions may not be what you expect. How will you deal with that?

Contemplate which is more important, your truth or your relationship? There are no easy answers, but consider what happens if you give up your truth because a friend can't handle it. Is that person really a friend if they ask you to give up your truth in order to remain friends?

It may actually be easier to start talking with strangers as there is less to lose. We did a chapter exercise on that earlier in the book. You might want to expand on that first before discussing your larger world view with your closest friends.

When you do start talking with your closest friends, you might want to present it as some ideas you are considering rather than as a new or deeply ingrained belief system. In that way you can back away and take it more gently if they are resistant at first. Remember that it has taken you a period of time to come to these insights. It is unreasonable to expect your friends to rapidly accept this whole new paradigm, shake off the carefully created disinformation and fear, and see the Cosmic Paradigm the way you do now after all the contemplation you have done as you read this book.

I think this exercise can give you huge insights into the problems our Star Cousins face in figuring out how to approach open contact with humanity. Then we have to consider whether they would be accepted or even safe moving openly among us at this time. You can help lay the groundwork to make that wonderful day possible much sooner. Your efforts will benefit humanity and be much appreciated by all when the truth becomes widely known.

MARY, MOTHER OF ET—BUILDING BRIDGES BETWEEN WORLDS

Note: When I started this chapter, my new acquaintance and soon to be friend Sierra Neblina was going through a lot of turmoil, trying to come to grips with what had happened to her and how to deal with it all as it unfolded. I had decided to use the catchy pseudonym "Mary" for her, in order to protect her privacy (You will have an "Oh Duh" moment in the 4th paragraph of this chapter). However, over the last year, she has been TOLD that now is the time to speak her truth boldly, and she has requested that I use her real name in this book. Her case is very complex and involved and is still evolving, but she knows that it is time to share her experiences, insights and knowledge of what is really going on in our world and our universe for the benefit of those ready to hear those messages. She has decided to do a book of her own on the whole story, and the messages and training as an Ascension Worker that she is still getting to this day. Thus you can consider this chapter to be a prequel overview of what she will be covering on her own in the very near future. I look forward to that book myself.

Awakened by a scream in the apartment courtyard and a bright light coming through the window, Sierra rolled over to check on her partner, who had gone to the bathroom. She noticed the clock (12:36 AM), and then noticed a small approximately 3 foot tall Grey ET in the room with her. She tried to move, but her body would not respond. This, of course, caused quite a fear response, but the entity seemed to be trying to calm her down and reassure her telepathically, telling her it was OK and that he would not hurt her. He proceeded to examine her and appeared to be making sure everything was fine with her medically. Several times, when things became too intense, Sierra would lose consciousness and wake up a little later. At one point, he scanned her with a blue light beam that felt physically cool, but what really weirded her out was that it felt *familiar*.

Flash forward, a friend of mine was visiting my area recently, attending a convention and visiting several friends while in town. Sierra, another friend of his, wanted him to see a movie that had brought back a flood of memories for her, and I was invited to tag along. The movie was called *The Fourth Kind*.

(Don't bother; it was a horrible horror movie.)

Over dinner after the movie, Sierra proceeded to tell us the rest of the story about the events described above, which had happened eighteen years prior. Back at the time of the encounter, when the examination ended and she could move again, she looked at the clock and over four hours had elapsed, with it now being 4:46 AM. At this point her partner Gina came hobbling out of the bathroom complaining that her, *um*, legs were asleep. She had apparently been frozen or asleep on the toilet for four hours. I'm sure you know the feeling. Gina had a friend visiting who was sleeping on the couch, and when this friend was awakened by the scream in the courtyard, she had gone to check on Sierra and Gina, who were in the bedroom. The last her friend remembers was raising her hand to knock on the bedroom door, and then she was waking up on the couch in the morning.

Well, first thing in the morning Sierra called a friend in the local psychic community. Her friend came right over, looked at her (or Sierra says it might be more accurate to say looked THROUGH her) and said, "You're Pregnant!" **"Not Likely!"** said Sierra, explaining that she was a lesbian and had NOT been with a man. Her psychic friend insisted, so Sierra got a home pregnancy test, and sure enough she was pregnant. In fact, she tried multiple home pregnancy tests of different brands, and they all came up positive. It is hard for anyone to imagine the range of emotions this caused for Sierra, and probably even harder for us guys. The psychic explained that these things generally ran in families, and encouraged Sierra to check with her mother. She did and found that there was an affair before she was born with a mysterious man that her mother had never told her about. This mystery man was working at a military base, and disappeared right after the affair in a way that made it impossible for her mother to contact him when she found she was pregnant. This mysterious and possibly non-human man is probably Sierra's father.

Over the next four months Sierra tested positive on the home pregnancy test. Sierra had determined early on to "Keep" the baby, and a circle of friends had helped her with psychic protection. However, one day she felt different, noticed her stomach was flat again, did another pregnancy test, and discovered she was now Un-Pregnant. Again, she had a swirl of motherly emotions as well as a lot of questions. Did she "lose" the baby, did she do something wrong, or was it now out there somewhere still alive? Now it was gone, and she was mad! During this time Sierra started doing a lot of research and digging, and this attracted the attention of the military. She had previously been on active duty in the Army but was a member of the inactive reserves at this time. So, not totally unexpected, she came home one day to find a black limo waiting for her.

"Get In" was the order. Sierra walked right over and said to the two Men in

Black types, **"It's About Time! I want some answers,"** and got in the back seat. In a way this was an affirmation that something real had happened to her. It was a relief that someone might have some answers for her, even though there was a bit of a concern about getting "disappeared." Sierra, who had been in her own words a real "Bad Ass" in the military, was in the last All Woman Brigade at Fort McClellan in July of 1990. She was the first woman to complete Patriot Missile School and become qualified to drive Patriot Missile trucks. Since that job description often involved being in front line combat zones or even behind enemy lines, she also qualified as a Sniper. She would park the Patriot Missile truck, stand off a ways, and keep an eye on things with the sniper rifle scope. She also was teaching Hand to Hand combat to the men. As they drove toward Cheyenne Mountain, a wide range of thoughts were going through her head, including the thought that she was trained and could take these guys out with a ballpoint pen.

Whenever she would get angry or consider the possibility of taking the guys out, the front seat passenger would calm her down telepathically. She now understands that he was a very gifted and evolved soul, possibly human, but most likely a hybrid or genetic experiment who was recruited in his youth for his psychic abilities.

Sierra was driven to Manitou Springs and the northernmost entrance to NORAD, which is an underground military base inside Cheyenne Mountain near Colorado Springs, Colorado. Once in the Mountain, the MIB took her to meet a geeky scientist who seemed very interested in her experiences. She was not eager to share all the details of her experiences at this time as she was still a bit confused and traumatized by it all, but the scientist finally said that he really wanted to know just one thing, did it communicate verbally or telepathically? Sierra said it communicated telepathically, and the scientist exclaimed, "I knew it!"

He showed her something right out of *Star Trek*, a device which transported inanimate objects from one chamber to another across the room. The Scientist had been drinking from a soda can. He placed that can in one chamber, asked Sierra to step behind a wall with a thick window, and pushed a button. The can disappeared from the first chamber and appeared in the second chamber. Sierra, having her wits about her enough to be skeptical, asked how she could be sure it was the same can. So the scientist scratched an X on the can and repeated the experiment. Sure enough, the transported soda can appeared with the X on it just as he had scratched it. Sierra did notice that he did not drink the remaining soda, at least before she left.

The MIB then took her on a tour inside Cheyenne Mountain and showed her a dead ET that was laid out on a table with a glass cover. (Except this one was about six feet tall, so in retrospect she thinks it was possibly a different species of Grey, since the one in her apartment was about three feet tall and seemed fully grown.)

Then she was taken deep into the Mountain and the MIB showed her a craft inside a cavern that was hovering in mid-air. It was some distance away, but Sierra was guessing it was about the size of a VW Beetle car. She could make out no markings to indicate if it was ours, but she got the impression that it wasn't. Neither the craft, the existence of ETs, nor the transporters are acknowledged by our government even 20 years later!

After the tour Sierra was taken to a conference room where she was pointed towards the chair at the end of a long conference table. She sat there for what seemed an eternity and finally, when she felt as if she might want to escape, a man in his early 60s, wearing a generic flight suit with no insignia but reeking of high ranking military intelligence sat down, looked at her a long time, then said, "Now that you know, **STOP DIGGING!**" What is a good soldier to do? So the incident slowly faded into the background for her over the years. At least until she saw that horrible movie.

As you can probably guess, that evening when I first met Sierra she was a bit out of sorts and trying to maintain her composure, but inside she was rather rattled and traumatized by the "Abduction" movie. She really needed someone to talk to! After dinner and some discussion of her story, we split up and went our separate ways, but within a few days Sierra wanted to meet me again. She was impressed that I listened without ridicule and offered some explanations and suggestions that made sense, and thus she wanted to talk to me some more. Sierra is very empathic, and had a strong sense that her "child" was trying to make contact with her.

We talked about how the Grey hybrid program was described by Bashar as technically not ET but rather a *parallel* Earth that had destroyed its environment. The inhabitants had had to adapt to survive and in the process they had lost their ability to procreate. In order for their species to survive, they had to come to Earth where many of the family lines were nearly identical in order to get genetic material for the hybridization program.

While I don't have any personal proof that this is true, I place a very high credibility on the Bashar materials channeled by Darryl Anka, not only because my intuition said that his information made sense and felt right to me, but also due to confirmation from Tashina[61]. Bashar had also indicated that, in most

---

[61]   Tashina had told me that Bashar made her homesick (for the 5th dimension), and that he was right on in his information, so I guess you could say that Bashar is ET approved.

cases, the human involved had made a soul contract agreement to participate in this program before being born into this body, even if they don't consciously remember it now.[62] Having some understanding of what may have been going on all those years ago helped Sierra find at least a point of reference.

Well, about a week later Sierra called me and said she needed to talk again. It was a little after noon and I suggested we meet for dinner, but she said she needed to talk—**NOW!** OK, I closed out the work I was doing and headed down the hill to her favorite restaurant to meet her. She said she was becoming very "controlling" about everything, and it was really bothering her partner. She didn't understand why she was experiencing this sudden shift in personality, but it was disturbing. So I asked if she felt like other aspects of her life were out of her control: the memories of the helpless feeling of being unable to move while being examined, the thought that she had a child out there in the universe somewhere and couldn't talk with it, and perhaps even worries that something similar might happen again.

Well, it didn't take Sierra very much time at all to understand that she was latching onto any aspect of her life that she thought she could control to compensate for those aspects she felt were out of her control, and this insight helped her a lot.

We also talked about how it is possible to change the terms of your soul contract if you wished, and that she could amend it in any way she wanted. I explained to Sierra that she could say or simply state her intention that *"I want nothing more to do with you"* or she could say, *"I will work with you, but on MY TERMS! You have to explain what you want to do, and I have to give my explicit conscious permission for each aspect of it before you proceed."* You can also state your intention that you wish to only work with entities that are working for the highest good of humanity. It is my understanding that even the less ethical ET groups have to honor your free will intention, and can no longer take a pre-birth soul contract as tacit approval to do as they wish. This second option is what Sierra chose, and she has subsequently maintained contact with a number of entities, but now on HER own terms[63]. As the

---

[62]   This view is also supported by GW Hardin in his fascinating radio interview on *The Timeline Wars*.
http://archives2010.gcnlive.com/Archives2010/may10/AmerikaNow/0529103.mp3
http://archives2010.gcnlive.com/Archives2010/may10/AmerikaNow/0529104.mp3

[63]   I strongly recommend this kind of intention setting to any of you who have similar events happening in your life that seem beyond your control.

relationships matured, they developed into a relationship with more mutual respect and openness. Thus a much more comfortable relationship has evolved, and with higher level entities than she was dealing with at the time of the first encounter in Colorado Springs.

The effect of this discussion was to leave Sierra feeling much more empowered about the whole situation, and she almost immediately stopped the out-of-character over-controlling behavior. She also felt that her child or someone was still trying to make contact with her, that she would feel a presence in her room at night, but she was unable to achieve full contact. As an empath Sierra had for most of her life been making contact with a variety of entities, primarily people who had recently passed through transition and wanted to leave a message for someone they left behind. Sierra was quite comfortable speaking with spirits and astral traveling, and thus being unable to make this connection with her own child was very frustrating for her.

Well, I believe it was that night I also had a strong impression of an entity or presence near me as I was falling asleep and again as I was waking up, but was unable to get more than an impression and no specific communications. I did get a strong impression that it was a daughter, and in an email to Sierra I wrote "Your Da.., uh child" (and explained that I had started to write Daughter like it was a Knowing). Sierra insisted that she felt it was a son or a male presence. I figured we would find out soon enough.

By chance (or perhaps not) that week I had a communication from Tashina, my friend who was (to the best of my knowledge) not born on this planet. In passing I mentioned what was going on with Sierra, and inquired if there might be some way she could help. Tashina reluctantly agreed, and we started making arrangements for her to connect with Sierra.

A couple of days later, Tashina got in touch again. Seems Sierra's "daughter" had shown up at Tashina's house in her young daughter's bedroom as an energetic but visible form. The little girl was attracted to the entity, but being half human she had been affected so much by the energy field that when she approached, the energy literally threw her across the room and she had sprained her ankle. Well, she of course called out to her mother, who came running to find the ankle obviously red and swelling already, and the entity apologizing profusely. Tashina went to get some ice for the ankle, and when she returned her young daughter said, "It's OK, Mommy, she healed me!"

Well, this was quite an interesting start, but Sierra's daughter proceeded to tell Tashina who she was and that her mission was to become a bridge between our two worlds. She explained that before she was born she was taken to a gathering of nine women and was allowed to choose who would be her mother, and she had chosen Sierra. She was now 12 in their time frame (18 Earth years) and when she became 18 she expected to be allowed to visit here physically. She also had some messages she wished to pass to her mother[64].

So I helped set up a phone call, explained to Tashina how to block caller ID to protect her identity, and set up a mutually agreeable time for her to call Sierra when Sierra would be waiting. All Sierra knew was Tashina's first name, that she had a special connection with her daughter, and to expect the call at the specific time. Well, the two women talked for two to three hours and had a marvelous time visiting, not only about Sierra's daughter, but also the larger picture of humanity and how we fit into the even bigger picture of our universe. Sierra was now much more at peace with the new paradigm and in acceptance of her role in it.

It is probable that the male presence Sierra was experiencing was the guide who she now feels was working on her for two years, preparing her for this time. He was very patient, rather like a gentle teacher or guide, who when she finally made good contact asked, "Are you ready?" She felt that this being was a facilitator of some kind, and after he had her prepared she was allowed to spend one night with her daughter. Sensing that this was a one-time meeting for now, Sierra stayed up until 7 AM sharing and getting acquainted with her daughter.

At first the energy was so intense, Sierra would get a body level "flight or fight" fear response, and that would pretty much shut things down. However, with practice she was able to make better connections. Sierra said that was unlike any astral travel or spirit contact she has ever experienced before, very strong vibrations and a disorienting shift of dimensions. She seemed to lose her point of reference, and still had some trouble with the physiological fear response. When she really connected, she said that after the vibrations there was a strong jolt, and it felt like her daughter's presence was inside of her, merged with her own. She was so far beyond where she had gone before that she had some fears about being able to get back, and her daughter asked, "What is that?" "Fear" was Sierra's telepathic reply. "Fear of what?" the daughter asked. "Death" was the closest Sierra could come up with. From the exchange Sierra felt that her daughter was not familiar with the emotion of fear, and that all emotions were probably relatively new to her.

During this encounter Sierra had been taking notes in a notebook in the dark, more of an automatic writing than consciously. At one point in the "conversation" Sierra had asked, "Who is this?" and the answer had been very hard to write down, taking a lot of extra effort rather than flowing naturally. The characters

---

[64] I'm guessing Sierra's daughter simply followed the chain of contacts until she found someone who was able to communicate with her across the dimensions.

that make what appears to be her daughter's name do not look like any Earth letters that I am familiar with. Sierra probably had to go to another level of interpretation than that which is our normal mode of letting pictures and impressions flow though into our normal language.

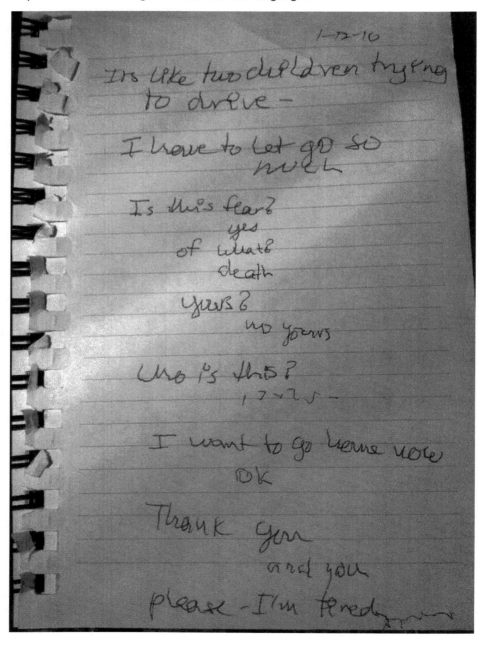

During that connection, Sierra and her daughter merged and communicated a little more easily as the night went on[65]. Sierra felt a very childlike presence of joy and play and the adventure of exploration.

Her daughter's name is virtually unpronounceable in our language. Sierra said it was more of an experiential feeling than a sound. She represented it as a symbol, and the best pronunciation Sierra can come up with is **Tucs' Ah Ee**, with a bit of a Navajo feel.

Asked what she liked to do, Sierra said watch movies. So they went to the living room and popped in a DVD. The daughter was quite enthralled with the human interaction and somewhat confused by the violence. Sierra did several pages of automatic writing in the dark during this encounter, and stayed up from midnight until 7 AM. After it was over, she was again quite exhausted, and within a day or two was sick with a combination viral and bacterial infection. We are not sure why, but we suspect that she was so physically drained, she was susceptible to infection because her resistance was way down. Sierra will have to learn to pace herself as she learns to interact with these different entities.

Later on Sierra started feeling a presence similar to a walk-in, but one that also "shared" her body rather than taking over. This entity seemed to be interested in preparing Sierra for the role she will play in helping the Ascension process with people, and also is giving her a number of insights into what is coming for humanity. There is a way that they establish an integration process where the other entities' consciousness is consciously live within Sierra's body, seeing through her eyes, and sharing but not taking over her body. In the process, Sierra is able to get a sense of what their culture and their lives are like. She got a sense of how small and insignificant this was in one way, but also sensed how much compassion they have for us at the same time. What was happening at that time, and continues to happen, is that there are small idiosyncrasies Sierra would notice, like how things tasted, or the way humans acted, or what she was thinking. There was the masculine

---

[65] Sierra's description of these encounters reminded me of the spontaneous shamanic journeys of Hank Wesselman described in his book trilogy *Spiritwalker, MedicineMaker*, and *VisionSeeker*, **http://www.sharedwisdom.com/** especially in the way that the two consciousnesses could coexist in one body for short periods of time. Perhaps with practice Sierra can learn to see her daughter's world through her eyes, and start to learn about them from that perspective. So far it has been the daughter exploring our world through Sierra's eyes.

energy that originally "Opened the Door" for her, and later she met a female entity[66] who was really stern and would often scold Sierra when she was having a human moment by feeling sorry for herself, and would say, "We don't have time for this." She explained that there was a flaw in our thought processes that was put into us a long time ago, but she was showing Sierra how to correct this flaw.

In one recent encounter while with friends, Sierra was asked to go up to the ship for very important training and her walk-in baby-sat her body while she was gone. Her body was still with her friends, but Sierra was totally on the ship for an important meeting. When she came back into her body, the walk-in had to brief her on what had happened in her "Absence." That was just a little strange, but Sierra is a real trouper and willing to experience a lot of high strangeness in order to fulfill her mission of helping educate humanity as to the larger paradigm and where we are headed.

Sierra continues to get more and more downloads that have to do with raising our consciousness, with physics, and even inter-dimensional travel. She is constantly getting blasts of new information, which she seems to be grounding in some way. They explain it as "52 critical mass," where if enough of us raise our consciousness to a sufficient level, it is like the 100th monkey, a domino effect or a tipping point where we reach critical mass and a shift occurs in humanity. Sierra is being given lessons that she is supposed to teach and share as widely as possible, and as quickly as possible. There is a sense of urgency that it is important for humanity to get with the program, and SOON![67]

---

[66]   Sierra feels this masculine entity has been working with her on a 24 hour basis for the last couple of years, and while glad Sierra was finally able to make the connections, was also impatient to get on with the training and with teaching Sierra what she needed to learn as rapidly as possible at this time.

[67]   There is much more constantly happening regarding Sierra's story, but I am also getting a strong push to get this book out SOON! The rest of Sierra's story will follow in another book specifically about her experiences.
http://www.blogtalkradio.com/starseed-radio-academy/2011/04/05/et-hybrids-and-government.mp3 (or .wma) Sierra starts her story at 11 minutes into the podcast.

WHAT IS NEXT FOR HUMANITY?

This is the Sixty Four trillion dollar question, and I have pondered over this for many, many hours. The simple answer is that I don't think anyone really knows. Some people see gloom and doom, others see Nirvana. Some have said that some species of ETs have been tampering with our timeline for their own reasons; others say that humans have developed time travel and teleportation in the covert projects and have been messing things up, or at least taking advantage of future information for personal gain. And then, while we believe the past to be relatively fixed (though it may not be as rigid as we presume), what is coming is more like a series of potential futures.

Then there is all the talk of the Shift, Ascension, or whatever you want to call it. Many feel we are entering a phase where the Earth is rising to a higher vibration due to a more energetic region of space we are entering, or due to Light and Love energies being beamed at us. We are supposed to be crossing the galactic equator and the photon belt in 2012, and that event seems to correspond with the Mayan calendars and many other ancient calendars like the Hindu Yuga's, or Long Years. Scientists had long wondered why the Milky Way appeared at a strange oblique angle in our night sky. Based on their theories, the spin of our solar system and our sun should match the plane of the galaxy. It was only recently that scientists had star photos over a sufficient time period (about 100 years) and instruments of enough accuracy that they could backtrack the motion of our star through the Milky Way galaxy and found that we orbit the galactic center at an angle. While right now we are very close to the galactic equator, in between crossings we oscillate a little above and below the equatorial plane of the Milky Way. What an incredible view that must be, to see the Milky Way from above[68]. But even more interesting, HOW did these ancient people all

---

[68] It is still debated as to how much of an angle we really orbit the Milky Way at, with with some saying we are actually part of the the Small Sagittarius dwarf galaxy that was captured by the Milky Way. In any event, based on ancient records and modern science we seem to periodically pass through different energetic regions of space and or different alignments of our solar system and the heavens that ancient cultures claimed had a profound effect on human events. Many systems, from Astrology to the Yuga's to the Mayan calendar, all seem to indicate that we are entering a new age at this very time. Most systems see it as a new golden age, and a very positive time to be alive. Use your creative abilities to make it the best possible change for humanity.

seem to know the date that we would next cross the galactic plane?

Gary Harden describes a condition he calls the Timeline Wars. Seems our reverse engineering of time travel technology opened our world up to visitation and manipulation by future humans who had vested interests in a couple of different timelines. According to Gary, we have, through our intention and focus on Unity Consciousness, broken free of the outside manipulation and potential destruction, and we are now creating our own future. The more we understand the fundamental oneness of all, the more powerful we become. If we collectively continue on this path, we are on the way to Nirvana, a higher dimension beyond the hate and fear that polarizes us now. As he says, "Something wonderful is going to happen, and we can't do anything about it." Gary is coming out with a new book about this very subject, and you can find information about this topic and his new book at: http://www.gwhardin.com/

This scenario fits well with my beliefs, intuition and knowing. As I have said throughout this book, you attract what you put out. Some say that no planet has ascended without help, and that we are surrounded by our cosmic brethren waiting for the appropriate time to make themselves known and to assist us. If you are personally and psychologically prepared, then this will be a joyous occasion, a meeting with long lost friends, and an exploration of our own potential. If we are brave enough to step beyond our comfort zone, we will find that as beings we are much more than we currently imagine. What is next for humanity is what you are creating with your own thoughts and actions right now! Move into oneness, community and unconditional love, become more heart centered, and that is what we can have as we co-create our new world. In light of my studies on this topic and my intuitions about it, another poem came flooding through very recently.

SHIFT

Planet in turmoil
Much is not the same,
Important to stay centered
This is not a game.

Winds are swirling
An absence of light,
Things might get scary
But avoid the urge toward
    flight,

For a few days
There will be severe tests,
If you can remain strong
Things will work out best.

When it is over
Many will find,
They have entered a world
Of a whole different kind.

No longer will we
Have to endlessly toil,
We will work for ourselves
Or work with the soil.

Our goals and objectives
Now will all be,
For the good of the planet
And of all Humanity.

Spiritual guides
Have always been near,
Once in the shadows
They are now abundantly
    clear.

Our jobs will change
Under this new Sun,
Life will be easier
And so much more fun.

We will find that
Given our druther,
Everyone chooses
To help one another.

Some will go back
to see if they can find,
Any of those
That got left behind.

Help them to see
What is right,
Encourage them to move
Into the light.

Others will work
With new technology,
Things that will make
Energy free!

Travel anywhere
With just a thought,
It's as easy as pie
With no ticket bought.

Meeting new peoples
We do with elation,
We make new friends
From all of creation.

Different dimensions
Even the Angelic realm,
Will soon be visible
Under our helm.

We learn to navigate
All that is there,
The people we meet
All treat us fair.

Gone is the darkness
Of duality,
There is no room here
For duplicity

Love and light
Pervade each day,
As we learn how to live
In a beautiful new way.

Past, present, future
Become a bit of a blur,
Living more in the moment
Is how things will occur.

A glorious uprising
Will occur in man,
A wondrous world to create,
We certainly can.

Living this way
Is certainly fun,
As closer to Source
We steadily become.

Challenges all around
That we look forward to,
A whole new world
Awaits me and you!

© 2011 Don Daniels

CONCLUSION

The Buddhists and Hindus are fond of saying Namasté. This word has multiple meanings, none of which translate well into English. One explanation, at least partially attributed to Ram Dass, that I think expresses this concept best is: *"I honor the place in you in which the entire Universe dwells, I honor the place in you which is of Love, of Integrity, of Wisdom and of Peace. When you are in that place in you, and I am in that place in me, we are One."*

That seems like a pretty nice place to be!

Dream big, think positive, keep looking inward, and make our future a good one. We are all counting on each other.

Don

APPENDIX A — REMOTE VIEWING

Remote viewing is a NATURAL ABILITY that we all have. It is probably quite common in our early youth, but especially in our culture it is "Trained" out of us as we grow older. Some cultures, like the Australian Aboriginal peoples, accept it as common and will talk about meeting another group at a certain trail crossing at a certain time, sometimes several days in the future. They call this ability "The Bush Telephone." Here there may be a fine crossover between what we call precognition and telepathy.

Some people I know use remote viewing as a form of intuition to avoid accidents or to find and assist those in need. One or two people I know are adept enough to operate on multiple levels of consciousness at once, and can remote view, looking for trouble ahead on the road as they drive. They can "See" what is ahead, be it an accident or obstruction, or even a police radar trap (saves money on radar detectors). I personally think these abilities are all very similar and closely related. Other closely related skills are psychometry (also called vibraturgy, the ability to pick up impressions by holding or touching an object) and precognitive dreams.

For your early experiments in Remote Viewing, you will need an assistant, preferably of the open-minded variety. You cannot place your own targets without knowing what they are. Ask your friend to place an object in a box and seal it for you. Then, when you are given the box, place it in front of you, do your basic meditation, go into oneness, become aware of awareness, and then just allow your awareness to focus on the object in the box. You can visualize the box disappearing, or visualize your consciousness going into the box, or whatever works for you. Then RELAX, don't try too hard, but simply be receptive to whatever impressions you might get. Write them down on a handy notepad or speak them into a voice recorder as they flow into your consciousness. Do not try to analyze at this stage, as the intellectual mind will shut down the intuitive flow. Just let the impressions flow and you can analyze later.

First impressions are almost always the most accurate, so after a while when you feel you are trying too hard or are no longer getting good pure impressions, end the session, open your eyes if closed, and write some notes about your impressions. Take a moment to analyze which observations seemed the strongest and most valid. Only after writing your raw impressions should you start to analyze and try to figure out what the target is. Then open the box and see how close you were, not just on the total object but also the various aspects of it, color, texture, shape, size, material, and even including emotions that may have been associated with the object by its owner. I find that metal or crystal objects tend to work best for me, paper and plastic do not seem to hold the vibrations as well, although sometimes very good results can be had using a map. Remember to correlate the location indicated on the map, and not just the picture on the map. Some people also use pictures in an envelope for targets, and that can work well also.

Some people get colors, sounds, emotions or feelings, a tactile sense of what the object is made of, or if you are lucky you might even have seen a clear picture of the target. I generally get sketchy, incomplete pictures which are sometimes combined with intuitions or emotions. It depends on whether you are wired more as a visual, auditory, kinesthetic or emotional learner, however most people will get some of all, so you can work on developing all aspects of your remote viewing.

The first couple of times you try this, it might be helpful if your assistant is across the room beyond the object, as you can pick up telepathic and non-verbal clues from them in the process. While these dilute the validity of a pure remote view experiment, when first practicing, you can use it to help correlate the feelings you get when you are right versus when you are wrong. Start to learn to trust that still small voice inside that never lies to you, and learn to differentiate it from the voice of the ego as well as the voice of the intellect. You can also take turns with your assistant, if they are willing and interested in doing the experiment also.

After a couple of tries, have the assistant sit behind you, so you no longer get the clues from their subtle body language, but you can still get telepathic clues when you say something that is right or wrong. Eventually you will want to go solo, and see if you can get good impressions without the assistance of another mind that knows what the target is. You can even go double blind where the object is packed by a third party and your assistant doesn't even know what the target is. If you want to totally eliminate the outside observer, try picking a place on a local map that you have never been, put an X or circle on that point, and try to get impressions of the site. Then physically go to the site and see how close you are.

Another way to practice when **riding** in a car on an unfamiliar road (don't try this when you are also driving) is to try to "See" what is ahead, around the next corner, for instance. You can also do this when walking, trying to see who or what is around the corner in the hallway or beyond the next bend in the path. I used to do a form of this as a kid on mountain roads, walking with my eyes closed for as far as possible and learning to trust that inner intuition. It might help to have a safety observer behind you, if there are hazards or drop-offs.

As you develop proficiency you can expand the complexity of the experiments. Arrange a time to "Visit" a friend, and describe what their surroundings look like, what they were doing at that time, and possibly a target that they have set up on the table for you. Or you can start adding in the dimension of Time, as in the higher realms time and distance are not the obstacles they are here in the 3rd dimension. An example is the remote view I had of the UFO sighting that was to happen out in Joshua Tree later the same night.

If you are not having decent success at this or just want to try something easier at first, try Psychometry. This works best if you have a small group of people and pair up with a stranger. Exchange objects that you frequently wear, like a watch, crystal or metal necklace, ring, or eyeglasses. Hold the object gently in your hand and do the basic meditation, becoming aware of awareness, and then simply become receptive to impressions that may flow in from the object. Again it is important to avoid trying to analyze at this time as intellectual analysis interferes with and often replaces the intuitive impressions you are trying to get. Speak the impressions as they flow in without filtering (agree beforehand to not laugh or ridicule each other, so you will not stifle the flow out of fear of embarrassment), and see what kind of impressions you get. I often get good impressions of a person's house and the area where they live.

Usually an object that has emotional significance to the person will store the vibrations of things that also have a strong emotional attachment to that person, like their home. I had a very good highly detailed and accurate RV of Emily Greer's home while holding her necklace. I "saw" a winding driveway with a circle drive, columns beside the front door, a detached multi-car garage off to the left which appeared to be for three or four cars, inside the front door you turned left to the kitchen, which had a tan or brown ceramic tile center island with something hanging over it which I took as one of those hanging pan and skillet holders. Out the back window there was grass, some bushes, more grass, and then dense trees.

Emily couldn't wait until I could visit so I could see how accurate I had been. The winding drive ended in a circle in the front yard. The detached multi-car garage was indeed off to the left of the house and held at least three cars. The kitchen was correctly to the left after entering the front door. The objects hanging over the center island in the kitchen were three hanging lamps and the color brown was a little off, but the view out the back window of the kitchen was very accurate. Emily pointed out that there were no columns by the front door. We were looking right at the front of the house, and I pointed out to her that there were indeed false columns beside the door, like large molding with a Roman column like bias relief. They were part of the front of the house, not freestanding like she had assumed. When I pointed them out, Emily realized that she had never noticed them as such before, but I had still picked up on them in my impressions. We were both astounded with the accuracy of the impressions I got from holding her necklace and letting the intuition flow.

Don't expect perfection at first, or even frequently, but with just a little practice you, too, can have some similar successes.

Doing these kinds of experiments for yourself will help provide direct experience and validation of how we are all connected in this holographic universe. Experiencing this personally changes your perspective from an intellectual curiosity to a personal knowing, and really deepens your understanding of and connection with "All That Is." In this way it will contribute significantly toward your growth and evolution as a Cosmic Human Being.

Have fun with it!

REFERENCES

CSETI: The Center for the Study of Extraterrestrial Intelligence. www.cseti.org

The Baca is the high desert near the Great Sand Dunes National Monument in the San Luis Valley, Colorado.

Dr. Steven Greer is the International director of CSETI, the Center for the Study of Extraterrestrial Intelligence www.cseti.org

Prime numbers are numbers that can only be divided by one and themselves: 1, 2, 3, 5, 7, 11, 13, 17, 19, 23...

Remote Viewing is a meditative technique whereby you extend your consciousness beyond your physical body in order to "see" or gain impressions from a remote location in space and or time. See Appendix a for a Remote Viewing exercise you can try yourself.

Rosicrucian Order, AMORC (Ancient Mystical Order Rosae Cruces) http://www.rosicrucian.org

One clue as to the reason for all the secrecy and disinformation: UFOs don't go zipping around the universe burning Exxon Jet A, and if we had their energy and propulsion systems, we would no longer be dependent upon the fossil fuel industry.

Dr. Greer says his contacts tell him the big bug eye lenses are like a combination sun glass/night vision lens to allow them to see in a wide range of lighting conditions, and are not their actual eyes.

Consciousness is considered by the Rosicrucians to be vibratory, operating on a very high frequency above sound, radio, and even the visible light spectrum. Just like the higher frequencies of Light are not limited to the speed of sound which vibrates at a much lower frequency, consciousness is not limited to the lower frequency speed of Light. Note how fast you can travel around the universe in your meditations.

DEEP SECRETS OF A UFO THINK TANK EXPOSED! by Anthony Bragalia
http://ufocon.blogspot.com/2009/07/deep-secrets-of-ufo-think-tank-exposed.html

I strongly recommend the Disclosure Project Video:
Disclosure. www.disclosureproject.org
It gives a lot of insight into the reasons for the secrecy and offers suggestions for how to help promote the disclosure of the truth on these issues. Also included on this DVD is a PDF file of the 500-page congressional briefing document, with blueprint drawings of the Flux Liner, leaked classified documents and numerous witness testimonies. This excerpt is from pages 358-366 of the Congressional Briefing Document, which EVERY member of the House and Senate received, hand delivered to their offices in May of 2001. This is the very same document you can obtain from the Disclosure Project.

The Missing Times—Terry Hansen (www.xlibris.com) or more specifically
http://www2.xlibris.com/bookstore/bookdisplay.asp?bookid=2313.

Faded Giant by Robert Salas, about the incident where UFOs apparently shut down some of our nuclear missiles.
http://www.ufopop.org/Special/FadedGiant.htm

Conan O'Brian's revenge: Proving that the media talking heads all get their marching orders from the same place.
http://www.youtube.com/watch?v=GME5nq_oSR4&feature=player_embedded

You can set up conference calls on Skype, Google Talk, or Microsoft Messenger that are free if everyone is using their computer and just a couple cents a minute to add phones. You can also use one of the free conference call services like www.FreeConferenceCall.com, www.FreeConference.com, or www.GoToMeeting.com/Conference-Call, where you generally only pay for your own toll call, but most cell phone plans are free on weekends, so have a blast.

See my website for photos of those pages from the Air Force Training Manual.
www.EvolutionThroughContact.com

If you prefer, you can start your contact attempts with a statement or intention that you wish to only work with entities of the highest ethics, those that are working in the Light and for the best interest of humanity and the Earth.

The Day After Roswell—Col. Phillip Corso

Bashar is a being of extraterrestrial origin, a friend from the future who has spoken for the past 26 years through channel Darryl Anka **www.bashar.org**

Tashina had told me that Bashar made her homesick (for the 5th dimension), and that he was right on in his information, so I guess you could say that Bashar is ET approved.

Adventures Beyond the Body http://www.out-of-body.com
Adventures Beyond the Body

Know Thyself: http://www.theosophy-nw.org/theosnw/world/med/me-elo.htm

Trillion, Decimal and *One. Trillion* was so similar to my experiences that I helped Mark Kimmel with Ideas and editing on the remaining two books. They are a great "Faction" (Fact based Action Adventure Science Fiction) read, and real page turners. **www.CosmicParadigm.com**

Tashina claimed to be from a 5th Dimensional world that we would not recognize, hence Tashina to better differentiate her from Sierra with a similar name.

Yes, you can touch them, they don't break! In fact, Tashina gave great hugs of appreciation for our help and understanding.

Mark Kimmel's latest book *Transformation* has a good description of the "Structures" we have allowed to control our lives, and some alternative ways from other civilizations. Easy to navigate by topic and in ebook download format, it is also very reasonably priced.
http://www.cosmicparadigm.com/Books/Transformation/
Also check out **http://cosmicparadigm.com/Athabantian/** for more current information as it comes in.

Consider the Arab Spring, the populist revolts in Europe, the Wisconsin recall elections in the US, and now public demonstrations all over the world demanding truth and honesty in government and business. It is already happening all around the world and increasingly here in the US where movements like Occupy Wall Street and Move Your Money are gaining momentum. It is just not widely reported by the corporate controlled press, who get their advertising revenue from these same big banks and corporations.

Some position papers by Dr. Steven Greer
http://www.cseti.org/position/greer/csetibrf.htm and
http://www.disclosureproject.org/docgallery.shtml

Rosicrucian Positio that speaks of other life in the universe.
http://rosicrucian.org/publications/positio.pdf

Yoko Ono created the World Peace Tower in Iceland in memory of John Lennon
and his efforts towards peace.   www.imaginepeacetower.com

A worldwide forum to discuss peace concepts. www.PeaceConsciousness.org

Some say our Nuclear weapons rip the very fabric of the Multiverse and affect
other worlds and dimensions as well as our own. If this is the case, it is an
even stronger argument to remove the scourge of nuclear war from the face
of the earth. Even if we think we have the right to destroy ourselves, do we
have the right to destroy parallel universes?

The Source Field Investigations, David Wilcock www.DivineCosmos.com

The view that the Greys are actually a Parallel Human group is also supported
by GW Hardin in his fascinating radio interview on *The Timeline Wars.*
http://archives2010.gcnlive.com/Archives2010/may10/AmerikaNow/0529103.mp3
http://archives2010.gcnlive.com/Archives2010/may10/AmerikaNow/0529104.mp3

Sierra's description of her encounters reminded me of the spontaneous shamanic
journeys of Hank Wesselman described in his book trilogy *Spiritwalker,*
MedicineMaker, and *VisionSeeker,* http://www.sharedwisdom.com/ especially
in the way that the two consciousnesses could coexist in one body for short
periods of time. Perhaps with practice Sierra can learn to see her daughter's
world through her eyes, and start to learn about them from that perspective.
So far it has been the daughter exploring our world through Sierra's eyes.

The rest of Sierra's story will follow in another book specifically about her
experiences. For the first part of her experiences, listen to her interview at:
http://www.blogtalkradio.com/starseed-radio-academy/2011/04/05/
et-hybrids-and-government.mp3 (or .wma)
Sierra starts her story at 11 minutes into the podcast.

EDUCATION, LEMURIAN STYLE

Students as teachers, an elder oversees.
Goals set for the season, the sooner done
the sooner the student for vacation leaves
work hard to learn, then go have fun.

The incentive is certainly there
To help tutor one another
Students really seem to care
And don't tolerate those who don't bother.

Slow in one topic, fast in another
Everyone needs to understand.
Tutor one subject, get help in the other
The class has to pass each subject demand.

No one goes it alone
Working together is the norm
Get the learning done
Then vacation the rest of the term.

© Don Daniels

This poem is based on others' channeled information about life and education in the ancient land of Lemuria.

MARS

Is there Life out there on Mars?
A planet very close to ours.
Or are we alone in this Universe?
If true, what an unkind curse.

Are there bacteria, plants, or even animals
among those dusty windswept Martian hills?
Some scientists now want to Bioengineer.
The effects on current residents are unclear.

One of the rovers keeps regaining power
the solar cells get cleaned in the midnight hour.
What mechanism cleans them when it is shady
we don't know, perhaps a Martian cleaning lady.

Mars is a planet of great mystery
Does it play a role in our ancient history?
Did our ancestors come from Mars,
or from further out among the Stars?

© Don Daniels

You may remember that the Mars Rovers were not expected to last more than a few months due to dust accumulation on the solar cells, reducing their effectiveness to the point where the rovers ran out of electrical power. They instead lasted for years, and on some occasions when they were really dirty and the controllers thought it was over, the solar cells would mysteriously be clean in the morning. There was a lot of speculation about how that happened, with the "scientific" speculation being that Martian dust devils had cleaned the dust off overnight. I have a little trouble with this as dust devils generally require uneven heating of the surface by sunlight to form, and generally don't happen at night. Also, I used to play in dust devils as a kid, trying to run into them on the school playground. I don't ever recall coming out cleaner than I went in.

EARTH DAY

On this planet Earth Day

Can show humanity the way

For us to stay!

That's all I have to say.

© 2004 Don Daniels

My shortest poem, but still says a lot!

.

RECOMMENDED LINKS

http://www.cosmicparadigm.com/

http://www.cosmicparadigm.com/institute-of-light/

http://divinecosmos.com/start-here/davids-blog/992-videooccupyyourself

http://www.masteringalchemy.com/

http://www.windstargalactichealing.com/

http://littlegrandmother.net/

http://www.starseedhotline.com/sierra.htm

http://www.bashar.org/

http://www.scientificexploration.org/

http://www.icehouse.net/john1/index11.html

http://www.cheniere.org/

I was privileged to meet Tashina several years ago, and it has been a truly mind expanding experience ever since. In fact, what I learned became part of my book *Evolution Through Contact—Becoming a Cosmic Citizen*. I know first-hand that Tashina is a very gifted healer and intuitive, so if you need help with major health issues or in finding your life purpose, I can recommend no better. Just remember that total honesty is the order of the day, as she will see right through anything less. If your intentions are pure, it can be an incredible personal growth experience.

Enjoy.

ABOUT THE AUTHOR

Don Daniels has always been one to explore outside the box. He was interested from youth in a variety of topics ranging from ESP to Cosmology to Nature and Science, to books about near-death experiences and life after life, to UFOs. Not content to just read, Don would experiment where possible. For instance, he built scale models of the pyramids and experimented with pyramid energy, managed to avoid any direct experience with Near Death, but does have a number of friends who did, and participated in UFO research outings. A commercial airline pilot by trade, Don has always had a wide variety of other interests as well. Don has been married to the same wonderful woman for 35 years and has two grown kids.

It was on his very first UFO research outing that Don had an experience that led to the writing of this book. A very high quality interactive UFO encounter occurred that night where the group flashed lights at the craft and it flashed back (and more)! This triggered a period of philosophical introspection into the meaning of other life in the universe and our place in that larger universe. This book takes you on that journey towards becoming a Cosmic Citizen, and includes simple exercises to help you become likewise, a Citizen of the Universe.

NOTE FROM DON: If you have had a UFO/ET encounter and after reading this book want to talk about it, you can contact me through the website www.EvolutionThroughContact.com or Consult@EvolutionThroughContact.com and we can arrange a time to talk.

I have been instructed by Adrial, a celestial, that it is very important that I make myself available to those readers who need a little more help dealing with their experiences. I would prefer that you complete the book first, if possible, so you have the full basis presented there to start from, but if you are having a crisis dealing with renewed memories, we can talk as you need.

19691740R00106

Made in the USA
Charleston, SC
07 June 2013